MW00441920

# The Health of Pond Fish

## By Dr. Herbert R. Axelrod

**Quarterly**

**yearBOOKS,INC.**
Dr. Herbert R. Axelrod,
*Founder & Chairman*

yearBOOKS are all photo composed, color separated and designed on Scitex equipment in Neptune, N.J. with the following staff:

**DIGITAL PRE-PRESS**
Patricia Northrup
*Supervisor*

Robert Onyrscuk
Jose Reyes

**COMPUTER ART**
Patti Escabi
Sandra Taylor Gale
Candida Moreira
Joanne Muzyka
Francine Shulman

**ADVERTISING SALES**
George Campbell
*National Advertising Manager*
Nancy S. Rivadeneira
*Advertising Sales Director*
Cheryl J. Blyth
*Advertising Account Manager*
Amy Manning
*Advertising Director*
Sandy Cutillo
*Advertising Coordinator*

©yearBOOKS, Inc.
1 TFH Plaza
Neptune, N.J. 07753
Completely manufactured in
Neptune, N.J.
USA

Cover design by Sherise Buhagiar

# Introduction

The selection of fishes kept in ponds, pools and lakes as pets and living decorations has resulted in the use of koi and goldfish as the primary animals. Consequently these two species of fishes have been selectively inbred to produce dozens of variations in color, body formation, scale appearance, fin shapes and lengths, eye protrusions, swimming abilities and behavioral characteristics. All of these varieties have resulted from genetic variations which might have been classified as *genetic diseases* and certain of these variations, like pop-eyes, celestial eyes and bubble-eyes in goldfish, would be treated as diseases if they appeared in koi.

Of course pop-eyes, for example, is usually a genetic variation in goldfish, but it can also be a symptom of a disease.

This book will help you to differentiate genetic variations from disease. It will also assist you in identifying and treating many of the diseases to which pond fishes are susceptible.

## What are Quarterlies?

Because keeping fish in ponds is growing at a rapid pace, information on the diseases of pond fish is vitally needed in the marketplace. Books, the usual way information of this sort is transmitted, can be too slow. Sometimes by the time the book is written and published, the material contained therein is a year or two old...and no new material has been added during that time. Only a book in magazine form can bring breaking stories and current information. A magazine is streamlined in production, so we have adopted certain magazine publishing techniques in the creation of this yearBOOK. Magazines also can be much cheaper than books because they are supported by advertising. To combine these assets into a great publication, we have issued this yearBOOK in both magazine and book format at different prices.

Distributed in the UNITED STATES to the Pet Trade by T.F.H. Publications, Inc., One T.F.H. Plaza, Neptune City, NJ 07753; in CANADA Rolf C. Hagen Inc., 3225 Sartelon St. Laurent-Montreal Quebec H4R 1E8; Pet Trade by H & L Pet Supplies Inc., 27 Kingston Crescent, Kitchener, Ontario N2B 2T6; in ENGLAND by T.F.H. Publications, PO Box 15, Waterlooville PO7 6BQ; in AUSTRALIA AND THE SOUTH PACIFIC by T.F.H. (Australia), Pty. Ltd., Box 149, Brookvale 2100 N.S.W., Australia; in NEW ZEALAND by Brooklands Aquarium Ltd. 5 McGiven Drive, New Plymouth, RD1 New Zealand; in SOUTH AFRICA, Rolf C. Hagen S.A. (PTY.) LTD. P.O. Box 201199, Durban North 4016, South Africa; in Japan by T.F.H. Publications, Japan—Jiro Tsuda, 10-12-3 Ohjidai, Sakura, Chiba 285, Japan. Published by T.F.H. Publications, Inc.

MANUFACTURED IN THE
UNITED STATES OF AMERICA
BY T.F.H. PUBLICATIONS, INC.

**CELSIUS° = 5/9 (F° − 32°)   FAHRENHEIT° = 9/5 C° + 32°**
**METRIC MEASURES AND EQUIVALENTS**
**CUSTOMARY U.S. MEASURES AND EQUIVALENTS**

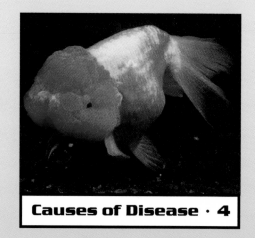

**Causes of Disease · 4**

| | | |
|---|---|---|
| 1 INCH (IN) | | = 2.54 CM |
| 1 FOOT (FT) | = 12 IN | = .3048 M |
| 1 YARD (YD) | = 3 FT | = .9144 M |
| 1 MILE (MI) | = 1760 YD | = 1.6093 KM |
| 1 NAUTICAL MILE | | = 1.152 MI   = 1.853 KM |

1 CUBIC INCH (IN$^3$)             = 16.387 CM$^3$
1 CUBIC FOOT (FT$^3$)             = 1728 IN$^3$   = .028 M$^3$
1 CUBIC YARD (YD$^3$)             = 27 FT$^3$   = .7646 M$^3$

1 FLUID OUNCE (FL OZ)             = 2.957 CL
1 LIQUID PINT (PT)= 16 FL OZ   = .4732 L
1 LIQUID QUART (QT)             = 2 PT   = .946 L
1 GALLON (GAL)   = 4 QT       = 3.7853 L

1 DRY PINT                       = .5506 L
1 BUSHEL (BU)   = 64 DRY PT   = 35.2381 L

1 OUNCE (OZ) = 437.5 GRAINS   = 28.35 G
1 POUND (LB) = 16 OZ           = .4536 KG
1 SHORT TON  = 2000 LB         = .9072 T
1 LONG TON   = 2240 LB         = 1.0161 T

**Fish & Plant Quarantine · 13**

1 SQUARE INCH (IN$^2$)             = 6.4516 CM$^2$
1 SQUARE FOOT (FT$^2$)           = 144 IN$^2$   = .093 M$^2$
1 SQUARE YARD (YD$^2$)           = 9 FT$^2$   = .8361 M$^2$
1 ACRE             = 4840 YD$^2$   = 4046.86 M$^2$
1 SQUARE MILE( MI$^2$)             = 640 ACRE         = 2.59 KM$^2$

1 MILLIMETER (MM)               = .0394 IN
1 CENTIMETER (CM)             = 10 MM   = .3937 IN
1 METER (M)         = 1000 MM   = 1.0936 YD
1 KILOMETER (KM)         = 1000 M   = .6214 MI

1 SQ CENTIMETER (CM$^2$)         = 100 MM$^2$         = .155 IN$^2$
1 SQ METER (M$^2$)     = 10,000 CM$^2$   = 1.196 YD$^2$
1 HECTARE (HA)     = 10,000 M$^2$   = 2.4711 ACRES
1 SQ KILOMETER (KM$^2$)         = 100 HA         = .3861 MI$^2$

1 MILLIGRAM (MG)             = .0154 GRAIN
1 GRAM (G)     = 1000 MG= .0353 OZ
1 KILOGRAM (KG)         = 1000 G         = 2.2046 LB
1 TONNE (T)     = 1000 KG = 1.1023 SHORT TONS
1 TONNE             = .9842 LONG TON

**Nutritional Diseases· 20**

1 CUBIC CENTIMETER (CM$^3$)         = .061 IN$^3$
1 CUBIC DECIMETER (DM$^3$)         = 1000 CM$^3$         = .353 FT$^3$
1 CUBIC METER (M$^3$)   = 1000 DM$^3$= 1.3079 YD$^3$
1 LITER (L)         = 1 DM$^3$   = .2642 GAL
1 HECTOLITER (HL)   = 100 L       = 2.8378 BU

# Contents

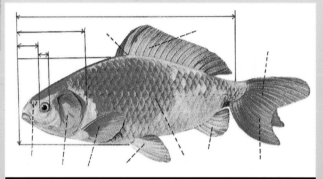

# Causes of Disease in Koi & Goldfish

Koi and goldfish can be called *pets* in the general sense of the term. They are animals for which we have developed a degree of affection. As such, we want them to be healthy and to live as long as possible. Prevention of disease is the key to success. In order to prevent disease you must supply your pond fishes with a healthy environment and good food.

**Water**

The basic environmental cause of disease of pond fishes is the quality of the water in which they are forced to survive. Whether you keep the fishes in a tank, man-made pond, natural pond or lake, the water must be suitable for their existence. Those characteristics which must be considered are temperature, pH (acidity or alkalinity), dissolved gases, dissolved chemicals, and such living things as algae, bacteria, protozoa and parasites.

Ideally, suitable water will be

The growth on the head of this goldfish is a desirable characteristic, as is the missing dorsal fin, but the growth is becoming so luxurious that the fish will soon be unable to see and probably unable to eat. It's too much of a good thing, but unless you know what normal is, you can't tell what is abnormal.

Unless you know what a healthy fish looks like, you can't evaluate a sick fish. This goldfish has normal nasal growths, but a close look indicates that the growth on the left side has a growth which is the beginning of a secondary fungus infection. An even closer look indicates that the gill cover on the left side is extended.

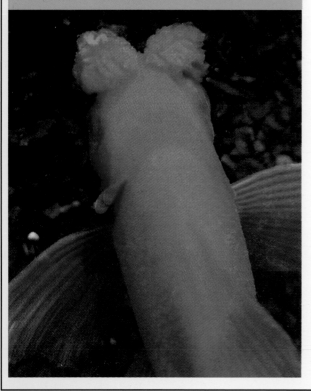

available for constant changes of the water by slow drip, slow flow or powerful filters. There is nothing as good for pond fishes as changes in their water. If water is not changed periodically, or perpetually via a drip system, the fish must live in its own excretion of bodily waste products like urine and feces, plus such gaseous wastes as carbon dioxide.

Most filtering systems handle the physical removal of waste via various mechanical sieves. The filter bed can be enhanced with huge surface-area enhancers upon which helpful bacteria convert biological waste (feces and urine) into harmless water-soluble chemicals. These filters assist in the control of ammonia. Ammonia is poisonous to all fishes and must be controlled by reducing it to a nitrate. Nitrates are beneficial to the growth of plants and are used as fertilizers in land crops. In the water they must not be allowed to build up, thus the need for water changes. During the conversion of ammonia to nitrates via beneficial bacteria, nitrite is produced. This intermediate chemical is very toxic and is responsible for many pond fish deaths.

The nitrogen-fixing bacteria, *Nitrosomonas*, are

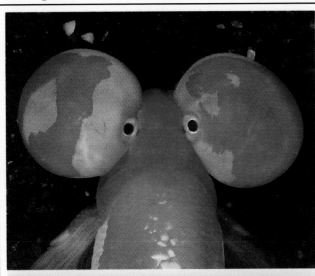

The bubble-eyes on this goldfish are a desirable characteristic. This fish also has celestial eyes...eyes that are always directed upwards. All bubble-eye goldfish eventually have problems with the weight of the fluid in the bubbles. The bubbles become so heavy that the fish can't swim.

The bacteria in the genus *Nitrobacter* change the nitrite to nitrate and the plants utilize some or all for their own growing needs when it combines with phosphates which are usually present in all water supplies (except rainwater). These same filtering systems also culture *Nitrobacter*, thus purifying the water when the whole system is in balance.

You must monitor the quality of your water with a suitable test kit which will give you fairly accurate readings of nitrites, nitrates, ammonia, and pH. You also need an accurate thermometer.

Simply stated, you cannot avert disaster without suitable monitoring equipment.

With a continuous supply of water at a suitable temperature and pH, you do not need a filter to control ammonia and nitrites.

**Oxygen**

While ammonia and nitrites are harmful and must be removed, oxygen is a necessary gas and must be provided. Usually enough oxygen is absorbed by the water directly from the air above the surface of the pond or tank. Suitable water movement created by the filter and an airstone will bring more water into contact with the air and not only will the oxygen be replaced, but the dangerous carbon dioxide will be released. Fishes (and people) can die from asphyxiation even in the presence of sufficient oxygen if their environment has too much carbon dioxide or carbon monoxide in it (the Bohr effect). The blood cannot

cultured in the filters on their exposed surfaces; thus efficient filters have mechanical means by which they increase the surfaces in their filter media on which the *Nitrosomonas* bacteria may be cultured. The use of a filtering system is not a guarantee that the poisonous nitrites and ammonia will be removed. As your fishes increase in size or numbers, they will produce more and more waste from their gills, kidneys and digestive processes. These waste products produce ammonia which the *Nitrosomonas* bacteria change to nitrites. As the temperature rises, so does chemical activity. Poisonous chemicals may be produced faster in warmer water as the waste products decay, and the filter which was sufficient under more normal circumstances may not be suitable for more fishes and higher temperatures.

This is a wonderful head growth, desirable because it does not interfere with the fish's eyes. If the fish is a prized specimen, like this one, it is not difficult to have the growth around the eyes surgically corrected. Eye surgery in prized fishes is already a common occurrence.

release the carbon monoxide or carbon dioxide quickly enough to enable it to absorb oxygen and carry it through the body. While ponds almost never suffer from carbon monoxide poisoning, they may suffer from oxygen depletion. Oxygen measuring equipment is available. A healthy pond or aquarium should have about 12 ppm (parts per million). Below 8 ppm and the fishes start having problems; at 3-4 ppm they start dying en masse.

Fishes under stress often rise to the surface and gasp for air by using the oxygen-rich surface water. But this usually is not enough in the long run (the Bohr effect) and the problem must be solved with immediate substantial water changes (25% within an hour; 100% within 24 hours). An emergency treatment is to add hydrogen peroxide to the water. Use the same hydrogen peroxide you use to sterilize minor cuts. It is freely available at every drug store (pet shops normally don't sell hydrogen peroxide). The normal size is usually 16 fluid ounces. Use one ounce per 10 gallons of water in your pond or tank. This will have an effect on your nitrogen-fixing bacteria, so turn off the filter while you are using this emergency treatment.

THE USE OF HYDROGEN PEROXIDE IS ONLY A FIRST AID, LIFE-SAVING TREATMENT WHEN THE FISH ARE DYING FROM LACK OF OXYGEN. In ponds it usually occurs when there is too much algae and cloudy weather prevents the plants from producing oxygen and absorbing carbon dioxide. Under conditions where the

light is too low for photosynthesis, plants give off carbon dioxide instead of absorbing it! For emphasis: IF THE FISH ARE GASPING FOR BREATH AT THE SURFACE OF THE WATER, THERE IS NO BETTER TREATMENT THAN CHANGING THE WATER. A HOSE SO DIRECTED AT THE SURFACE OF THE POND OR POOL THAT IT CREATES THE MOST WATER MOVEMENT IS MOST DESIRABLE AND SHOULD CURE THE PROBLEM ALMOST IMMEDIATELY (WITHIN 24 HOURS).

## pH

The measure of alkalinity and acidity of water (or any liquid for that matter) is called the pH. The p stands for an arithmetic designation meaning *number*. The H stands for the hydrogen ion. So pH is a measure of the hydrogen ions in the water. pH kits are inexpensive and pH can be controlled in aquariums and ponds with various chemical additives.

When koi or goldfish are gasping for air and staying near the surface, they are either feeding or in severe stress. Photo by MP&C Piednoir Aqua Press.

These additives accumulate and must be flushed out with periodic water changes. A very necessary part of your aquarium equipment should be a water changer which simply hooks up to a faucet. It has a 50 feet long (or maybe more) hose which connects the gadget to your tank. It removes water as it replaces it, taking all the trouble out of water changing.

Koi and goldfish are very hardy fishes which readily tolerate water temperatures from freezing to almost 85°F. An ideal temperature is probably 60°F., though it is impossible to control the temperature at this precise level either in a pool or in a pond.

Pond fish (koi especially), do best in water which has a pH of neutral (7.0) to 7.5. They easily tolerate a range from 6.0 to 8.0. What does affect them as far as pH goes is the chemical imbalance when the pH changes too quickly. This is especially true when the pH drops on the acid side. Fortunately, chemicals to raise the pH are safer and easier to use than chemicals which make the water more acid. Simple baking soda can change the pH to the alkaline side when it is too acid. Simply add a little at a time, waiting 15 minutes for it to dissolve before you measure the pH again. Add only as much as is absolutely necessary. If acidity is a problem with your home water supply (it rarely is because it will eventually dissolve your metal plumbing!), you can consider adding crushed coral sand or broken clam or oyster shells to the pond, pool or aquarium.

Submersible filters that combine mechanical, chemical and biological filtering functions in one unit are available for use in garden ponds. In addition to improving the looks of the ponds in which they're used by making the water clearer, they also make them more habitable for the fish by removing or neutrtalizing harmful substances from the water. Photo courtesy of Energy Savers.

If it occurs in a very large body of water you must treat the water with stronger alkalis such as sodium hydroxide. But this is dangerous and certainly not for the beginner.

**Temperature**

Koi and goldfish can live under ice, but they will die if their pond is frozen solid. Koi stop feeding when the water is about 50°F. Goldfish feed until the water drops close to freezing. So stop feeding when these temperatures restrict the appetites of your fishes.

While the water temperatures between freezing (32°F) and 85°F accommodate both koi and goldfish, changes in temperatures can be dangerous. Temperature shocks to colder water are the problem.

If you buy some koi or goldfish in a pet shop which has a temperature of about 70°F and you dump them into your pond which has a temperature of 40°F, you can expect to lose the fish. But if you took pond fish from water at 40°F and put them immediately into 70°F, you probably won't have any trouble. To be on the safe side, keep your fishes in water which changes temperatures slowly. Thus if you have an aquarium and the heater breaks, you want to be sure that the water doesn't get too cold too quickly, even if you have to add pots of very hot water (CAREFULLY!!!!) by slowly broadcasting it over the surface of the aquarium.

Sudden temperature changes also affect the nitrogen-fixing bacteria in your filter, too. So keep an eye on your filter's efficiency with your ammonia and nitrite test kit.

**Poisoning**

Ponds, pools and aquariums are all subject to

introduced poisoning. The subject of treating ponds, pools and aquariums with too much, too many or incorrect remedies, such as dyes (iodine, mercurochrome or potassium permanganate), are all poisonings under the control of the hobbyist.

Almost all garden ponds and pools are adversely affected by the random treatment of adjacent lands with herbicides and fertilizers. It is usual that well maintained gardens are regularly treated with poisons (herbicides) to control weeds. The application of these weed-killers is usually accomplished with a spreader which disperses herbicide powder or liquid over the grass or crops which may be in close proximity to the garden pond or pool. Winds easily carry these poisons into the garden pond or pool where they may cause the death of all the fishes contained in these bodies of water.

The application of these herbicides need not be in your own garden or farm. It can be from an area close by when there is a strong wind which is capable of carrying the poison into your pond or pool. Thus it might be wise to advise your neighbors of the potential hazard so YOU can be warned. When advised of the threat from neighbors, you have several methods of protecting your fishes. Obviously, covering your pond with large sheets of vinyl or polyethylene plastic is the best protection. Running your available water supply at full force is a second defense. The changing of water is almost always good for any pond. You can run the water while the pond is covered with plastic, too.

If your garden pond is heavily covered with floating plants, the effects of the herbicide poisoning might not be apparent until rain washes the herbicide off your plants into your pond. Thus covering

Natural fish ponds are lovely and practical ways to drain lowland areas and prevent them from becoming swamps. Care must be taken that the run-off from the adjacent lands does not contain pesticides, herbicides or fertilizer. Photo by Franz Hay courtesy of *Aquarium Live* from Bede Verlag.

with plastic is really the best way to go. The herbicide might kill your aquatic plants, too, and if these decay they can create havoc in your water garden. Obviously all dead and dying plants must be removed as quickly as possible even as you change the water.

Requesting that your neighbors wait for a windless day is less dependable.

While herbicides are almost always a fatal disaster for a pond or pool, fertilizers are usually not as dangerous. At most they change the pH of the water and increase the food available for algae, thus causing an algal bloom which might rob the water of sufficient oxygen to cause stress to the fishes affected. The plastic sheeting is helpful, but changing the water is also extremely efficient in countering the effects of fertilizers falling into your pond or pool.

Rarely wild and domesticated animals fall into a pond and drown, causing pollution of the water with their decaying bodies. This may happen when you are on holiday and no one watches your pond.

Larger ponds also may have visits from migrating water fowl. Their droppings may affect the quality of the water with increased bacterial activity caused by the organic and liquid droppings of the visiting water fowl. Occasionally, these water fowl may be covered with insecticide or fertilizer which they might have picked up from walking or resting on freshly treated grass. Most water gardeners welcome these attractive ducks and

**This magnificent fish pond receives water from rain runoff in a local intermittent stream. Rain runoff can carry many undesirable chemicals which might poison the pond.**

geese, barely recognizing the potential problems their visits might bring with them.

If you live in an area where aerial spraying against gypsy moths or mosquitoes is practiced, your problem is more complicated. In these cases you have to search out the source of these services and request them to advise you of their activities in proximity to your water garden. This is never an easy task but such companies which do aerial spraying are usually localized, so a search of your local telephone directory and a few pertinent telephone calls might be in

order. By putting your notice to the companies in writing, you will get more serious attention, for then the sprayers might have a legal liability for the damage they may cause to your fishes.

The final warning is about the application of algicides. These are chemicals which are used to keep the algae from growing onto the walls of swimming pools, and to keep the water free of algae which turn the water pea-soup green. Weaker concentrations of these chemicals (usually chlorine-based) have been used to clear ponds and pools

BEFORE fishes or plants are introduced. Never use them when fishes or plants are in the pool. There are algicides which are available from pet shops (like copper sulfate). They are effective when properly handled and most are based upon an *accurate* knowledge of the amount of water in your pond. Such knowledge is important because knowing the exact volume or exact weight of the water in your pond is necessary to put in the proper amount of chemical. If algae are a problem, your most successful control is with an ultra-violet (UV) sterilizer. These are easily obtained from your local pet supplier. The size of the sterilizer depends upon the size of your pond, the amount of over-feeding you practice (this is fertilizer!), the temperature of your pond water, the amount of plant-cover which cuts down on the amount of light assisting the algae to grow, the number of

fishes you have and the amount of money you are prepared to spend. Larger units are best. They can be run for shorter periods of time and, when there is an algal bloom, their full strength might be needed. One thing to keep in mind with UV sterilization is that the bulbs get weaker and weaker with each use and need replacing periodically. They usually have a useful life of 2,000 hours, but check this information on the unit you buy, or contact the manufacturer and ask him. Rarely do the pet shop personnel know what an *MWS* is. This is a micro-watt-second and denotes the power of the unit. To control algae you need 35,000-40,000 MWS. UV sterilizers are also suitable for controlling parasites, but then you need much more powerful units. Controlling parasites with UV is not practical for the water gardener.

Ultra-violet germicidal energy is superior for killing algae, bacteria and protozoa exposed to its rays. It can keep any water garden crystal clear when properly used. Photo courtesy of Aquatic Eco-Systems, Inc.

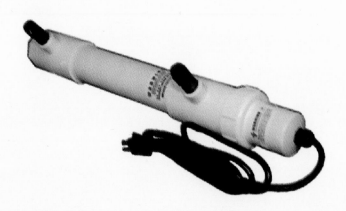

### Chlorine

A few words about chlorine. Chlorine is almost always added to municipal supplies of drinking water. The chlorine is used to kill bacteria. Too much can kill fishes and kill humans, too. The author has used water straight from the tap AS A

WATER CHANGE for more than 50 years and has never had a chlorine poisoning problem. If you change 25% of your pond water daily and you use tap water at the acceptable temperature, you should not have any problem with chlorine. Pet shops sell a dechlorinator chemical known as sodium thiosulfate. This can remove chlorine successfully. Instructions for its use come with the chemical. For treating a pond, you need this chemical by the pound. Many water garden specialists sell this in bags

Fishes gasping at the top of a pond indicate serious trouble. Add fresh running water as a spray as quickly as possible!

This lovely water garden in Singapore enables the fishes to be observed and fed from the center of the pond. When building a wooden bridge, take care that the wood has not been treated with poisonous (for fishes) chemicals. Photo by Dr. Herbert R. Axelrod.

In a Japanese hotel, small fish ponds are used to decorate the ground floor window areas and to guarantee some privacy. The top of the pond is 80% covered with plants to insure that algae do not become a problem. Photo by Dr. Herbert R. Axelrod.

from 5 to 50 pounds. Follow the instructions carefully. Usually it is best to fill up the new pond with fresh tap water and allow the chlorine gas to escape naturally, aided by strong aeration.

Fluorine is a chemical usually added to municipal tap water supplies to assist in combating tooth decay. While it potentially may be poisonous to fishes and plants, there is no reliable report of this having ever occurred. There are chemicals available from your pet supplier or water garden

center to control fluorine in water destined for your aquarium or pond.

Adding fresh water from the tap to established pond water is even better because 100% fresh water takes time to *age*. The process of aging allows the bacteria to bloom causing cloudy water during the first few days, but then it disappears and is usually safe for fish. To test that the water is safe for fish, buy a few common goldfish and put them into a small container (a plastic bag will do) which contains the water from the pond. If the fish live for 3 days it will usually be safe to add larger fishes. In any case, add fishes and plants to your pond or garden pool judiciously...one or two a day. Don't forget to quarantine your fishes and plants BEFORE you add them to your pond! (More about quarantine in the next chapter.)

# HIGHLIGHTS IN THE CONTROL OF DISEASES IN POND FISH

1. Ideally, constant small water changes create the best environment for goldfish and koi. A 5% water change every day, uniformly throughout the day and night, is best.

2. Controlling ammonia in the water, created by decaying waste matter excreted by the fishes, is an absolute necessity.

3. You must regularly monitor the quality of your water with suitable test kits. Once a week is enough if your fish are not showing signs of stress.

4. Sudden drops in water temperature are extremely dangerous to fishes.

5. Ponds can be poisoned by insecticides, herbicides and fertilizers applied to adjacent areas.

6. Try to calculate the exact amount of water, by weight and volume, in your pond, pool or aquarium. Any high school geometry student can do this for you. Water weighs about 8.25 pounds per gallon.

7. Algae are best controlled with an ultra-violet (UV) sterilizer to which a filter is attached.

8. Before putting fishes into a new pond, the water must be tested with inexpensive common goldfish.

9. NOTHING is more important to the health of your fishes than the water in which they live.

Both fishes and plants MUST be quarantined to insure that they are not a vector in bringing parasites or harmful microscopic organisms into your aquarium, pond or water garden. This quarantine, by the way, applies to bringing new houseplants into your home, or adding more birds to your aviary. It is simply a very vital thing you can do to PREVENT health problems.

### Handling Pond Fishes

Keep in mind that although goldfish and koi are very hardy fishes, they still suffer stress and possible injury when being netted, handled and moved. Torn scales and fins are the usual results of netting and handling. They are easily visible. But stress and internal injuries are not easily observed. Only the results of internal injuries may be observed; unless wounds heal easily, they may become infected with the usual fungus attacking the tissues killed by the bacterial infection. You must learn how to net and handle fishes. This can only be done with proper nets. The nets must be large enough but not too large (better too large than too small). Chasing a fish around a garden pool with a small dip net is not only comical, it can be tragic, because you lose patience and become more aggressive.

Often you must actually catch the fish to treat it, take a sample of a parasite, inject it or observe it more closely. This should always be done with WET hands. Dry hands will result in the removal of the protective slime coating which every fish has, thus

Frequently it is safer for the fish to be picked up with wet hands than to be netted. At the annual koi show in Tokyo, Japan, most of the larger koi are handled in this manner. Photo courtesy of RINKO magazine.

opening a site for infection. There are possible (very rare) cases of humans becoming infected from using their bare hands in aquariums and garden ponds. These usually have been traced to being wounded or cut in the encounter so your body's protective skin has allowed a pathogen to enter. Be careful!

Removing the fish from a net must also be carefully done. Don't simply dump the fish into a shallow holding tank and hope for the best.

Yoshiko Adachi, a California koi farmer, shows the proper way to net a large koi. You must use a shallow net and dump the fish quickly into a larger container for further disposition. Photo courtesy of RINKO magazine.

Placing the netted fish into the holding container should be done with the fish never being completely out of water. Photo courtesy of RINKO magazine.

Fishes can be stunned by the fall if they hit the solid bottom of the tank.

In catching the fish...good luck. Catching fish in a large body of water is not easy, and that's one of the problems with treating pond fish diseases. Observing them for parasites is also a problem. The most practical solution is to hand feed the fishes and observe them during feeding. Just the fact that they don't come to feed (assuming they came before) is a reason to consider them to be behaving abnormally and thus possibly ill.

To catch a particular fish in your garden pond, you might try two large nets. One net is held still while the other drives the fish into the stationary net. Once you get used to it the problem of netting fishes is lessened. In an aquarium, of course, catching a fish is easier, but it may be complicated with aquarium plants and decorations.

Like any other technique, netting a fish takes practice, common sense and proper nets to make netting as stress-less as possible. Stress can kill a fish. The signs of stress are hiding, swimming abnormally, cessation of eating, cessation of reproduction and finally death. You must remove all stressful situations from your fish's environment. That's what this whole book is all about. Stress, of course, comes from diseases and parasites, too.

### THE HOLDING TANK

In order to properly quarantine a fish you must supply it with a suitable environment, one that is large enough for comfort and small enough to enable you to observe its health. These observations are based upon your ability to recognize external parasites and other health problems which cause the fish to swim or behave abnormally. As individual diseases are discussed later on in this book, the appearance of parasites and abnormal swimming behavior will be defined. There is no sense in having a holding (quarantine) tank if you cannot recognize an affected fish.

The holding tank can also be used as a hospital tank when the occasion arises. While holding tanks usually do not require heating, hospital tanks usually do require heating.

The holding tank can also be used to hold baby fish which may appear in the early summer after your fishes may have spawned. Healthy, mature koi almost always spawn in the spring when the water temperature hits about 65°F.

There really is no special product on the market called a HOLDING TANK. You have

Koi netted from the large ponds in Japan are carried tightly packed in small containers. They are placed under terrible stress during these netting, carrying and transporting operations and must be medically treated before they are sold or transferred to another pond. Photo courtesy of RINKO magazine.

When the author lived in Japan (1950-1952), koi and goldfish were transported in wooden containers like this one. Eventually they were replaced by plastic bags and cardboard boxes. Photo courtesy of RINKO magazine.

to make your own, buy your own, or build another small pond or pool in which new fishes and plants can be quarantined. In all cases, the holding tank must be shallow so you can observe the fishes and plants closely. It must also be covered to protect fishes from jumping out and prevent them from being abused by kids, snakes, cats, birds and thieves.

The holding tank used by the author is a children's pool. It is made of plastic and is about 4 feet in diameter and 18 inches high. It deflates when not in use and is easily stored. It must always be clean, so keep it protected when not in use. From the point of view of fish maintenance this kind of holding tank is too shallow, but deeper tanks make observation more difficult and the whole purpose of a quarantine is to be able to ascertain whether your new fish has parasites that are visible or behavior which is inconsistent with normal swimming and posture. Use a strong flashlight when examining the fishes in your holding tank. It makes it easier to recognize a parasitic problem.

The holding tank must be protected from the sun so it does not overheat. It requires aeration via an air stone and filtration with the common sponge filters which are available from any pet supplier.

The water in the holding tank should be aged. It can be treated with a weak methylene blue solution. The amount of methylene blue to add as a prophylactic can be determined by the

The ideal holding tank is about 100 gallons, lightweight and easily sterilized, covered, aerated and heated.

instructions that come with this dye. The water should be a light blue. This treatment affects the viability of biological filtration.

Non-iodized salt, like kosher salt, should be added to the holding tank. Salt is undoubtedly the best cure-all because it kills more parasites than any other single SAFE chemical. It is safer since pond fish have a greater tolerance to slight over-dosing. It is usually not toxic to people (unless you swallow a lot of it), and it is very inexpensive. It normally does not kill the bacteria in your filtering system and is relatively easy to administer. A dosage of 0.025% is recommended for the holding tank. That means if you have 100 gallons of water in your holding tank (which weighs 825 pounds), you need slightly more than 2 pounds of salt. Dissolve the salt in hot water before adding it to your holding tank. Add the salt a few days before you put fish into the tank. Remember that the salt stays in the water even if the water evaporates, thus building up the strength of the salt solution. So replace water which evaporates with fresh water. Do not add any more salt as it is cumulative.

Fishes in your holding tank are stressed and they will not act normally for a day or two. Floating a piece of styrofoam on top of the holding tank, covering not more than 25%

Dr. Tsai, a famous Taiwanese koi lover, shows his holding tank. It floats in a larger pool of water to maintain the proper temperature. Photo courtesy of RINKO magazine.

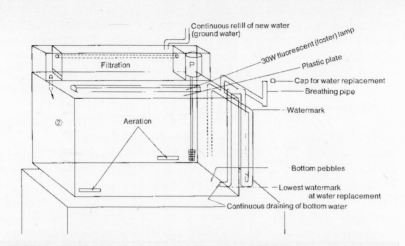

Continuous refill of new water
(ground water)

30W fluorescent (foster) lamp

Filtration

Plastic plate

P

Cap for water replacement

Breathing pipe

Watermark

Aeration

②

Bottom pebbles

Lowest watermark
at water replacement

Continuous draining of bottom water

The ideal hospital (quarantine, holding) tank has a filter, aerators, lights, heaters, etc. This drawing is the kind recommended by Japanese koi lovers. They don't believe in using heaters. Drawing by Shigehiko Inagaki, RINKO magazine.

The shallow containers used by most koi aficionados for displaying their koi at shows and fairs are excellent for quarantine tanks for small fish and aquatic plants. Photo courtesy of RINKO magazine.

of the surface, allows them shade and shadow. They usually like to hide under this protection. You should also have a large piece of plastic pipe in the holding tank. It should be as long as the fish and 50% larger in diameter than the fish's height. Fish will often hide in the pipe when they are stressed.

Other chemicals, like water soluble tetracycline or terramycin, can also be added at about 250 mg (the capsules usually are 250 mg each) per each 5 gallons EVERY TWO OR THREE DAYS, but then you must change 25% of the water in the holding tank every time you add the tetracycline.

Basically you do not need to add drugs (chemicals) to

This garden pond has been allowed to become badly overgrown on both its surface and at its margins. In addition to being unsightly, rampant plant growth also can have a bad effect on the health of the fish living in the pond.

your holding tank if the fish were healthy to begin with. Carefully inspecting them before you buy them is the best protection.

REMEMBER THIS: Most fish drugs and chemicals are poison. The idea is to kill the parasites and not kill the host (the fish are the host). Every drug or chemical treatment is stressful to the fish so the less drugs and chemicals you use, the better it is for the fishes. Fishes which are very sick, being unable to swim or having a body almost covered with ulcers, with torn fins and lying on their sides or floating on the top of the water, are best humanely destroyed with an overdose of fish anaesthesia or fast decapitation. Treating sick fish in your holding tank requires sterilization of the holding tank after use. This is best done with chlorine bleach added to the water before you empty the holding tank. Allow the holding tank to dry out before adding new water. Be sure to leave the heater, filter and air stone in with the bleach so they too are sterilized. BE SURE TO UNPLUG THE HEATER BEFORE THE STERILIZATION AND EMPTYING PROCEDURES. Your heater should be rated at about 5 watts per gallon of water you expect to warm. The temperature in the holding tank should SLOWLY be raised to 80°F once the fish are put into it. This will cause the eggs of some parasites (like Ich) to hatch, making them exposed to the salt and methylene blue which will kill the parasites in their free-swimming adult form.

The ideal holding tank is a

Koi gather at the fresh-water inlet to get oxygenated water when they are suffering oxygen starvation. Photo courtesy of RINKO magazine.

100 gallon aquarium, but these are expensive and require suitable stands, lights, etc. But if you have such a tank available, use it.

**Sterilizing Plants**

Plants must be sterilized before they are added to your tank, pond or pool. Sterilization of plants is simple. You can use the holding tank, of course, and lower the water level. More simply, a plastic garbage bag can be used. Measure out 20 gallons of water and add 5 drops of formalin to the bag. Allow the plants to stay immersed for 5-6 hours. This will kill all parasites, snail eggs and fish eggs which may be attached to the plants. Be sure the plants are TOTALLY immersed in this formalin bath. If some plants are sticking out of the water, the whole sterilization procedure might be ineffective. After sterilizing the plants in the formalin bath, the plants MUST be rinsed in fresh running water for a few minutes to remove all traces of the formalin. Formalin is VERY poisonous to fishes even though it is not very poisonous to plants.

# FISH AND PLANT QUARANTINE HIGHLIGHTS

1. Torn fins and other wounds caused by netting or any other reason must be protected from bacterial infection and subsequent fungus attack. Simply smear the area with a cotton swap and the same tincture of iodine you would use if you cut your own finger.

2. You usually can't treat a fish if you can't catch it. This is especially true of treating fishes for wounds and parasites and other maladies that might require application of a medication directly to the body of the fish instead of being broadcast throughout the water..

3. Only handle fishes when your hands are wet. Dry hands remove the fish's slime coating.

4. Use two large nets to catch fish.

5. Stress kills fish. The progressive signs of stress are abnormal swimming, cessation of reproduction, cessation of eating and death.

6. If you have a garden pond, pool or aquarium you must always have a holding tank of about 100 gallons handy for acclimatizing new fishes, quarantining new fishes and plants, and treating individual fishes for disease.

7. The holding tank must have a heater and sponge filter. Be sure to sterilize the holding tank after each use with chlorine bleach.
Unplug the heater before you empty the holding tank.

8. Sterilize water plants with 5 drops of formalin per 20 gallons of water for 5-6 hours to kill any parasites, fish eggs or snail eggs they may be harboring.

There are two types of nutritional problems. One is feeding your pond fishes with foods which are poisonous and which kill your fishes quickly. The other is long-term malnutrition caused by feeding unbalanced diets. It usually takes two years for fishes to be killed by malnutrition.

## POISONOUS FEEDS

Not infrequently koi foods are exposed to poisons introduced to them by accident. A poisoned rat may die in with the open bag of koi feed. Sprays against insects may settle on an open container of koi feed. Your hands may be invisibly coated with soap residues which can come off on the feed when you handle it. Almost all of these accidental contaminations of koi feed can be protected against by carefully sealing the containers in which the feed is stored after use.

The additional feeding of fresh greens such as lettuce, spinach, carrot tops and the like are perfectly edible by koi but they might contain fertilizer or insecticide residue which can affect your fish's health. If you boil these greens for a minute before feeding, you will make them easier for the fish to eat and will have dissolved all the chemical residues which might be on them. Even washing them under running water for a minute can be very helpful.

Unquestionably, goldfish and koi enjoy greens and they may be vital to their heath. The way the author supplies his koi and goldfish, kept in the pond, with greens is to plant the pond fairly heavily

This group of hikari-moyomono (3-colored koi with metallic scales) are all prize winners exhibiting perfect body shape. The heavier fish is a female heavy with eggs. Photo courtesy of RINKO magazine.

with water lilies. The lilies are planted in large pots and, as the shoots arise from the tubers, the fish eat them. Of course this means you'll never see a water lily or leaf thereof floating on the top of the water, but at least you'll have healthy fish. You can raise some of the water lilies to flower by protecting them with screens until the leaves reach the water's surface.

## NUTRITIONAL DEFICIENCIES

Unfortunately, many of the feeds available for pond fish are merely feeds intended for trout or catfish. These feeds, though readily acceptable by pond fish, will in the long run cause serious problems.

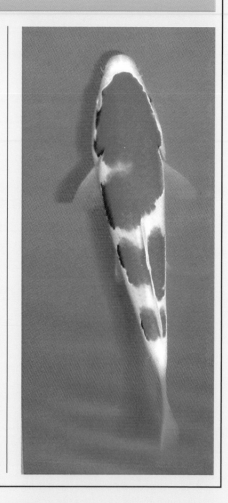

This kohaku koi (two colors), is much too thin for an adult fish, and is developing razorback, a nutritional disease.

The health of captive pond fish is directly related to the quality of care given them. Active, good-looking fish like these koi can only be the product of sound feeding and pond management techniques. Photo by Dr. Herbert R. Axelrod.

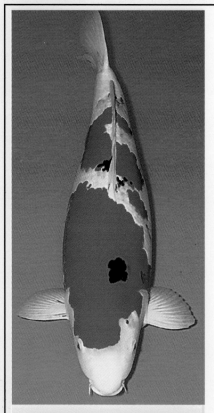

**This taisho sanshoku koi is a large champion-quality fish heavy with spawn but also suffering from fatty liver.**

Koi require vitamins in the same manner as most other vertebrate animals (humans included). The most fatal of these vitamin deficiencies is Vitamin C. A shortage of Vitamin C results in the fish getting musculature contractions which cause its body to bend into an S-shape. Fortunately this is a reversible condition if observed in time. Kinking bodies may be caused by many other factors such as a sharp punch to the body by another fish, a blow from a netting attempt or a poorly administered injection. Many poisons (like malathion) can also cause the body to kink.

Two kinds of kinking bodies are recognized. They are caused by spinal curvature. *Scoliosis* is a lateral curva-ture. When the fish is ob-served from above it looks like it has an S curve. When viewed from the side it looks normal. On the other hand *lordosis* is a spinal curvature from front to back. It causes the fish to have a hunch-backed look. While these conditions are treatable, the results are poor. There are many genetic causes of kinking and these, of course, are not curable but may be passed on from generation to generation.

Most claims in koi feeds list *VITAMIN C ADDED*. Vitamin C may also be listed as ascorbic acid in one form or another. Unfortunately, by the time you use these ascorbic acid-enriched feeds, the Vitamin C has lost its potency and is completely useless. Certainly within 6 months the Vitamin C will have lost its usefulness and you have no idea how long the feed has been on your dealer's shelf !

A version of stabilized Vitamin C is available on the market, but this, too, has a short shelf life (less than one year) and again you don't know how long it has been sitting in the container. Unfortunately, the date of manufacture is not required marking on koi or goldfish feed packages. But stabilized Vitamin C is better than nothing! If possible look for the name ASCORBYL-2-PHOSPHATE. This form of ascorbic acid is stabilized Vitamin C and is almost completely utilized by koi and goldfish.

Fish foods packaged in air-tight containers, to which Ascorbyl-2-Phosphate has been added, may be consid-ered as having usable Vitamin C until the package is opened. Once open, the food in the package begins to deteriorate. For this reason don't make too large a bulk purchase of fish food.

**Fatty Liver**

A common nutritional disease is fatty liver degenera-tion. Almost all fishes that overeat have some form of fatty liver problems. Fatty liver is curable situation by an abrupt change in diet and more exercise. This means giving the fish more water movement so they continually have to fight against the water current.

**When a fish bulges on one side, it is usually a tumor in the abdomen, rather than fatty liver degeneration.**

Koi and goldfish with fatty liver degeneration look full and plump, but they are actually on a course to death. If a koi or goldfish dies while it looks plump, do an autopsy and check the liver. If you find the belly full of fat and the liver discolored from its normal dark red color, you can be certain it had a bad diet and succumbed to fatty liver degeneration. In almost all cases this is due to feeding fishes on a diet of excess fat and poor quality protein. If you check the contents of the feed and find that it is basi-cally corn, or potato based, you are using the wrong feed. Stop using it immediately. You don't want to offer too much vegetable protein to fishes over the long term.

The best feeds are based on fish protein. Of course a pound of fish costs much more than a pound of corn, so expect to pay more for fish-based protein. Be sure that the feed you offer contains the stabilized Vitamin C in the form of Ascorbyl-2-Phosphate. The author feeds uncooked saltwater fish available at the local market. The saltwater fish is ground, bones and all, like chopped meat and fed to the koi. Sometimes they don't take this aggressively, but if you don't feed them for a few days, they'll be more eager to eat it. Since both koi and goldfish are bottom feeders, don't worry about it sinking. Fish protein diets will make your fishes much more colorful, too.

If you find a fatty liver degeneration, increase the water changes to a minimum of 25% per week and feed the chopped fish. The bones of the fish supply vital calcium to fast-growing fishes.

# HIGHLIGHTS: NUTRITIONAL PROBLEMS

**1. Poison foods can kill fish quickly. Fresh greens might contain herbicides, insecticides or fertilizers. (Fertilizers dissolved in the water usually don't kill the fish, but fertilizers eaten as plant residue easily can.) Wash all greens under running water before feeding them to your fish. If your fish begin to die for no apparent reason, suspect food poisoning and START CHANGING THE WATER FAST. CHANGE THE FOOD EVEN FASTER.**

**2. The Vitamin C that pond fishes require to survive is provided in a stabilized form in some modern fish foods. Such food must be packed in airtight containers. The food in opened containers starts to deteriorate.**

**3. Fish bodies can become kinked sideways or front to back as a result of poor diet, abrupt temperature changes or heredity. If you see such kinking, change the diet and the water—but realize that these measures might not help.**

**4. Feeding pond fishes cereal-based foods designed for other species will put unwanted fat onto them and cause fatty livers, verifiable only by autopsy. If an autopsy of a dead plump fish shows a belly full of fat, act fast. Immediately change the diet of the remaining fishes to ground-up marine fish, bones and all.**

**5. There is nothing better than live *Daphnia* and brine shrimp to supplement a diet of prepared food. But these foods are not cheap.**

# The Balanced Aquarium Myth

Fishes give off droppings. The droppings are good plant fertilizer for aquatic plants. During their respiration, fishes take in oxygen from the water and exhale carbon dioxide. Plants need carbon dioxide to grow. As the plants grow, they remove the droppings in one form or another, and give off oxygen. All of these statements are true and, theoretically, if there are enough fishes and enough plants, the aquarium or pond should be in balance.

HOWEVER, plants only use the droppings and carbon dioxide in sunlight. That's when the chlorophyll they contain converts these items into usable starches which the plants use for their growth. When there is no sun, at night for example, the process reverses. The plants give off carbon dioxide and absorb oxygen, competing with the fishes. Too much carbon dioxide may create the Bohr affect which will suffocate the fishes in the pond or aquarium. It might also affect the pH of the water since the carbon dioxide forms carbonic acid and this makes the pH drop, perhaps enough to create an acid condition which is dangerous to koi and goldfish.

So the balance between plants and fishes is a myth. You MUST have additional mechanical support systems to rid the water of excess carbon dioxide while at the same time adding depleted oxygen. This is simply done with running water, air stones and filters which bring the bottom layers of water up to the top where the exchange of gases (carbon dioxide out, oxygen in) takes place.

Most pond fishes do best in planted aquariums and ponds, even though these celestial goldfish probably never see the bottom of the pond. Not only do growing plants serve as food for the fishes, but the fish lay their eggs among the vegetation, the fry hide among the vegetation, and the algae are better controlled when they must compete with larger plants for the nutrition within the water. Photo by Burkhard Kahl.

Here Water Hyacinths are growing in profusion and helping to keep the water clear by both competing with the algae for available plant nutrients and shading the pool. The hyacinths themselves, however, can become pests if their growth is left completely unchecked. Photo by Mary Sweeney.

This book is not a book about plants; there are books about planting your koi and goldfish pond. Get them from your local pet shop. A list of all fish and plant books is usually included in *Tropical Fish Hobbyist* magazine (the publishers of this book also publish that magazine).

### ALGAE

While almost all aquatic plants are good for the garden pond, some of the small ones are not. These small plants are called *algae*. Not only are they unsightly, possibly turning the pond or aquarium into what looks like a container of pea soup, but they can give off huge amounts of carbon dioxide when they do not have enough sunlight (though artificial lighting is possible).

Small, single-celled algae are good feed for baby fishes (less than one month old); having some green cast to your pond during the spring breeding season is not altogether a bad thing. But when the sun gets hotter and the days longer, the light green coloring gets darker and darker until you can't see anything in your pond. It is, therefore, better to be prepared to control the growth of algae in your garden pond.

There are three ways to control algae growth: chemicals, UV sterilization and light protection. Let's discuss the pros and cons of each of them.

### CONTROLLING ALGAE WITH CHEMICALS

There are two basic types of algae which inhabit a garden pond. There are long filamentous algae which grow on

This magnificent pond, artificially created by Dr. Tsai in Taiwan, can be kept clear of algae with UV filters. The use of chemicals is fine for killing the algae but it is dangerous for the fishes. Photo courtesy of RINKO.

**Fishes living in this pea soup algae pond are barely visible. This kind of water is good for spawning (the baby fish eat the microscopic animals and plants), but injured or sick fish cannot be recognized. Photo by Dr. Herbert R. Axelrod.**

*Using chemicals to control algae is the least desirable method available.*

**Light Protection**

Algae need light to grow as do all green plants. By restricting the amount of light that falls onto the pond's surface, you reduce the ability of the algae to reproduce and sustain growth. The usual two ways light is obstructed from the pond's surface is by building a shade structure like a gazebo over the pond, or by growing floating water plants like Water Hyacinth or Water Lettuce so that about 50% of the surface of the pond is covered. These fast-growing water plants must be continuously thinned out as they grow very quickly. They normally double in size every week when the sun is strong. There are smaller floating plants like duckweed, *Lemna* and the like, but once they get into your pond they are hard to remove.

Submerged plants like *Elodea, Myriophyllum* and *Cabomba* are also effective in robbing the algae of light and nutrients, but they are difficult to control and quickly fill the pond unless the fishes eat their tender shoots.

PLANTS MUST BE STERILIZED BEFORE BEING INTRODUCED INTO THE POND. They frequently carry disease organisms, often in the form of eggs or spores, and may harbor adult worms, snails and their eggs, or even fish eggs. This is especially true of the *bunch plants* such as *Cabomba, Myriophyllum* and *Elodea.* Sterilization of plants is simple. Merely obtain some formalin from a veterinarian, undertaker or chemical

plants and from the sides of the pond wall, and the unicellular algae which cause the pea soup condition. Algae require fertilizers (foods) which contains phosphates and nitrates. In order to control the algae chemically, you have to remove all or most of the nitrates and phosphoric compounds. This isn't easy but is doable by sufficient running water. The fresh water contains no nitrates, so the algae starve to death while being flushed out with the changing water. This changing water is excellent for the fishes' health, so this is a highly recommended way to control algae. Such chemicals as copper sulfate can also be used. Copper sulfate is dangerous, as you might overdose the pond. There are several formulae by which you can calculate the amount of copper sulfate to add to your pond. None of the formulae

are fool-proof as the copper sulfate required is totally dependent upon the TOTAL ALKALINITY of your pond water. Thus, you have to measure the total alkalinity with a special test kit and get a reading in parts per million. Then you divide this parts per million reading by 100 and that figure will give you the required dosage of copper sulfate required in parts per million. This calculation isn't easy nor are the measurements necessarily easy either.

If you are able to remove all the fish from the pond, you can easily treat the water with chlorine bleach to kill all the algae (and anything else in the pond as well!). Then by aerating vigorously, the chlorine gases off. A chlorine test kit will indicate when the water is safe for the fishes, or, better yet, change 100% of the water.

supply house, and add 5 drops to 20 gallons of water. Soak the plants in this solution for 5-6 hours, rinse them off in fresh running water, and you can safely put them into the pond. This sterilization is very effective but handle the formalin with care. It is especially dangerous for your eyes and is extremely dangerous to drink. Breathing in the fumes of formalin is also unhealthy and uncomfortable. If you don't want to use formalin, try potassium permanganate. This purple dye is much less toxic, has no odor and has a wide spectrum of uses and concentrations. Using a white bucket, add enough of this purple dye so you can't see the bottom. Soak the plants in this for 3 hours, wash them off in running water and then introduce them into your pond. Potassium permanganate is a strong dye and it might color your fingernails purple if your hands are exposed too long. Using sodium bisulfite, you can remove the purple stains. By the way, if you have athlete's feet, potassium permanganate will give you relief if you soak your feet in it for an hour.

### UV STERILIZER

You can easily disregard ALL the above suggestions for algae control by using a UV sterilizer with attached filter to capture the killed algae. UV rays are dangerous to your eyes. They come in a sealed tube through which the water is pumped. The speed of the water and the strength of the UV rays are what determines the time and energy necessary to control the algae. Using the

proper strength of the UV sterilizing tube guarantees the destruction of all unicellular algae (that's the kind that makes the *pea soup*).

Each UV sterilizer comes with complete instructions. Follow these instructions carefully. Keep in mind that a harmful by-product of UV sterilization is that the water slowly becomes heated. The UV tubes produce tremendous heat along with the UV rays. Don't even touch one to see if it's hot. Pull out the plug and wait an hour or more before you handle it.

The usual UV tubes have a usable life of about 2,000 hours. That's about 85 days of continuous use. This usually is sufficient to take care of the bright, warm summer season. Change the tubes every year (assuming you only use it three months per year). Algae usually are not a problem when the temperature drops below 60°F.

Changing the filter that comes with the UV sterilizer is very important as a clogged filter might impede the flow of water through the UV circuit and render it ineffective.

Simply put, there is NO better method of algae control.

The claims of some UV sterilizers that they kill all parasites is usually boastful. The amount of energy you need to kill algae might be about 35,000 micro-watt-seconds. To kill parasites, bacteria and other undesirables, you need at least three times that much!

Using the UV filter requires your bringing a safe source of electricity to your pond. This is the job of a professional electrician. Don't try to do it yourself. The resulting shocks might injure or kill you and your fishes. A koi subjected to severe electrical shock can quickly die or develop a kinked back; it usually makes futile attempts to rise from the bottom.

A well balanced drainage pond has been made into a koi pond. The water lilies and other aquatic plants provide enough shade to protect against an algae bloom. Photo by Patti Ann LaFetra.

Left open to the sun, the water in this pool has become heavily populated with one-celled algae that have imparted their green color. Photo by M. P. and C. Piednoir, AQUA PRESS.

# NOTES ABOUT THE BALANCED AQUARIUM MYTH

1. Balancing fishes' waste in the form of droppings and carbon dioxide respiration with a plant's need for carbon dioxide and fertilizer (droppings) is a myth because it is impossible to have a balance between fishes and plants.

2. Plants are very useful with pond fishes because the fishes eat the plants, stay in the shade of the plants, spawn in the plants and the health of the plants is often indicative of the suitability of the pond water for fishes.

3. Aquatic plants denude the pond water of nutrients necessary for algae to thrive.

4. Algae can be controlled by chemicals, shade and UV sterilization, along with the use of additional aquatic plants.

5. By far the best method of algae control is to kill the algae in the pond water and filter out the dead algae. UV sterilizers are available from your local pet supplier to do this job.

6. UV sterilizers also can kill parasites and bacteria, but the strength needed is at least three times the strength needed to kill algae.

7. When using a UV sterilizer or any other electrical equipment, guard against electrocution of yourself and the fish. Severe electrical shock in fishes often results in kinked bodies.

# The Anatomy of Pond Fishes and How to Recognize Fish Diseases

As we talk about fish diseases, we will constantly be using simple technical terms to describe where and how the problems are expressed by the fishes. Therefore it is necessary to learn the essential body parts of a typical fish like a koi or goldfish. Many goldfish have had their fins enlarged, reduced or removed by the preservation of mutant genetic variations expressed in the varieties we often refer to as *fancy goldfish*. In koi we have had variations only in fin length, colors and scale formations. More variation will, undoubtedly, follow. In

The Japanese koi officials only recognize certain colors and combinations of color. This beautiful new strain of long-finned koi is forbidden entry into Japanese koi shows. Photo by David LaFever, Blue Ridge Fish Farms.

## EXTERNAL ANATOMY OF A TYPICAL GOLDFISH OR KOI

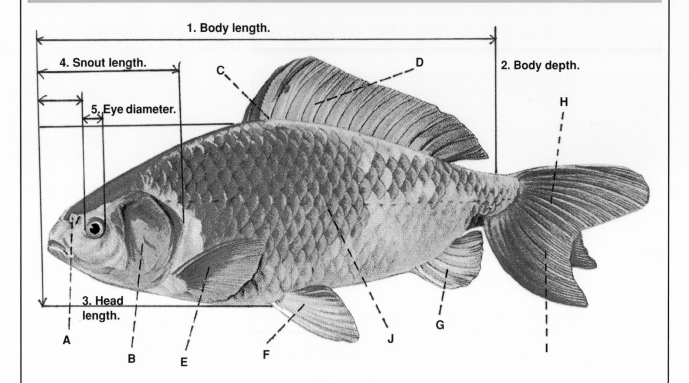

1. Body length. 2. Body depth. 4. Snout length. 5. Eye diameter. 3. Head length.

A. Narial fold. B. Gill cover. C. Spiny ray of dorsal fin. D. Dorsal fin. E. Pectoral fin. F. Ventral fin. G. Anal fin. H. Upper lobe of caudal fin or tail. I. Lower lobe of caudal fin or tail. J. Lateral line.

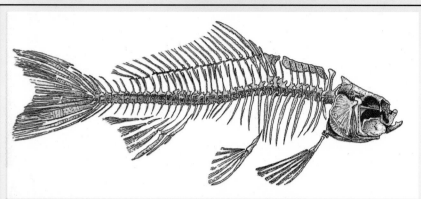

**Drawing of the skeleton of a koi (carp). Drawn by John Quinn.**

**An actual koi (carp) skeleton. Photo by Dr. Herbert R. Axelrod.**

**Koi are schooling fish. They usually stay together when swimming. If a fish does not swim with the school there is a good chance the fish is either sick or injured. Photo by Burkhard Kahl.**

Japan, the home of the colored version of the carp we call koi, any variation in fin length has been rejected, as have other physical peculiarities. Only color variations are accepted and even many of them have been rejected from competitions or else lumped into a mixed class they call *kawarimono*.

## ABNORMAL BODY PARTS AND BODILY FUNCTIONS

The only way we know that our pond fish are sick is to observe them. When we observe parasites, wounds or torn fins, we can readily acknowledge something is wrong. Usually by the time an inexperienced water gardener recognizes a fish is sick, it is too late to treat it.

Essentially, the treatment of fish diseases relates to the treatment of an individual fish. Treating a pond filled with fishes with drugs or chemicals is usually impossible from a practical point of view. When the whole pond is under siege you have to find the cause and not try to treat the symptoms. If you cannot define the health problem, you cannot solve it.

Here are the symptoms of fish health problems.

### The Body Surface

The most simple health problem to diagnose is parasitism. All fishes are subject to fish parasites. The usual external parasites are *Ichthyophthirius*, *Lernaea* and *Argulus*. *Lernaea*, and other common fish external parasites, will be more thoroughly discussed in the next chapter. Such parasites can be seen, and the fish's behavior changes. It slows

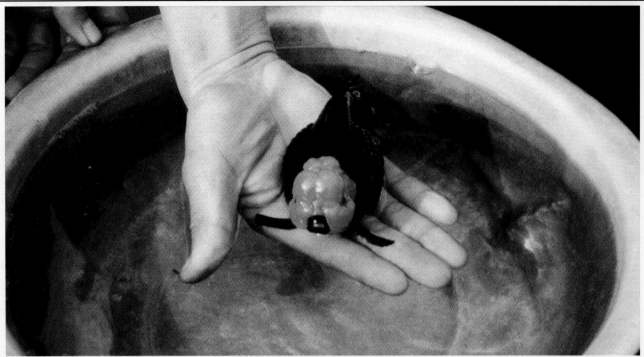

Above: This is pure magnificence. A solid black fish with a red lion head cap and pearl scales! Unless you know what a normal fish looks like you might not appreciate this gem!

Below: This very odd fish, black and white, split double tail, bulging eyes and no dorsal fin, is a new Chinese variety. It is extremely valuable for breeding. But, unless you know about fishes, you won't know what a fish like this is doing in your pond filled with bred-in-spring baby fishes.

A floating plastic hose, connected to make a ring, is used to confine floating plants in the author's pond. Photo by Evelyn Theresa Axelrod.

A full view of the author's pond with the lilies at one end and the floating plants at the other. This 50% surface coverage plus the UV filter keeps the water immaculately clear. Photos by Evelyn Theresa Axelrod.

down a bit, starts to lose the luster of its bright colors, and the outer skin's protective slime coating begins to slough off.

It is necessary to catch the fish and have the parasite(s) identified and the fish treated in the holding tank (quarantine tank). You usually do not need an expert to identify the problem if you have a simple magnifying lens and have finished studying this book.

**Unsocial Behavior**

Koi are schooling fish. In large pools, lakes and ponds, they swim in a tight formation like a flock of ducks. Only healthy koi swim in groups; sick koi are unable to keep up with the group and eventually they fall to the bottom before they float (dead) to the surface of the water. These sick fish get progressively worse as they lose their health. They often swim in circles, try vainly to rise to the top, bang their faces or bodies against the wall as though they were blind, and finally, they lose all energy and cannot escape your hand when you pick them up.

There is, however, a social structure amongst fish suffering from infestation of *Argulus* and *Lernaea*. These fish group themselves in tight formation at a bottom corner of the pond.

Rapid massive changes of water up to 50% per day usually solve the problem. The weaker fish are those which suffer the most when the water environment begins to go bad.

Koi do sleep. They usually rest on the bottom of the pond with their pectoral fins closed.

Sick koi, on the other hand, lie on the bottom with their pectoral fins open. At this stage they are still able to dodge your hand if you try to catch them, but they only move a short distance before they sink to the bottom again. They are usually unable to escape a net. After a few days of this kind of behavior, they die. A water change will not help these koi.

**Breathing and Eating**

Watching your healthy koi will give you the impression of the frequency with which they open and close their mouths. Let's call this *breathing*. The opening and closing brings fresh water over their gills where the fish is able to get rid of the carbon dioxide waste and exchange it for oxygen. The surface of the gills is very extensive (almost equal to the total surface area of the fish itself!) in order for it to execute this vital process. When the gills fail in their efficiency for any reason, or if there is insufficient oxygen available (or too much carbon dioxide), the fish stay at the surface of the water breathing very hard..like they are out of breath. A massive water change with water agitation is the first aid for this symptom. Usually the whole pool population goes through this stress at the same time.

You have to catch a specimen to examine its gills. If there are parasites, or the gills are congested and sticky, this is a serious gill disease problem which will be discussed later.

When the fish loses its appetite, that is the first major sign of a stressful situation and the fish should

This new variety just popped up as a genetic mutant. It has a red base to all the fins, red, bulging eyes, a white body and a nice disposition.

This new variety has nasal growths which have prevented it from eating.

This fish is a handful! Its eyes have been saved by surgery in the growths around the head and the lower jaw.

A chocolate brown goldfish with an upturned head is one of the newer results of Chinese goldfish breeding.

paste out of it with water. To this paste you add the antibiotic in the desired strength. Then dry out the paste and crumble it. If you have a spaghetti maker, then make spaghetti from the paste, allow it to dry, break it into suitable size and offer it to your sick koi. All the fish in the pond can be treated in this manner.

Pet shops often sell medicated food but you have to be sure the medication is the drug which you need and at the proper strength.

### Site Wound Treatment

If a fish gets wounded, cut, bitten or injured in such a way that the skin is broken, the wound can be treated in the same way that you would treat your own wound. Peroxide, iodine, mercurochrome, cortisone,

be watched carefully. If its excrement is abnormal, the fish must be removed to the holding or quarantine tank for treatment. Constant water changes usually help in this situation, but an antibiotic treatment may be necessary.

### METHODS OF TREATING SYMPTOMS OF FISH DISEASES

There are five methods of treating sick fish: oral administration, at-site wound treatment, medicated bath,injections and operations.

### Oral Administration

Basically, oral administration is accomplished by adding drugs to the food. This is done by first deciding which drug to use after completing your physical examination of the sick fish. Then you buy some regular koi food and make a

How ideal! If you can feed your fish from your hand, like this, you can feed them medicated food when necessary, and closely observe them for parasites, injuries or diseases! Photo by Michael Gilroy.

You must know normal fish behavior to understand when the fishes act abnormally. These fish could be dangerously short of oxygen...or rushing to get fed if they have been trained to come for their food. Photo courtesy of Peter Cole and Audrey Baschet originally published in Aquarium Life via Bede Verlag.

# MEDICATED BATHS FOR KOI AND GOLDFISH

The times and dosages suggested are just guides since such factors as size, age of the fish and its physical condition all contribute to the success of the medicated bath. In all cases remove the fish to aged water if there are any signs of discomfort.

| DRUG OR CHEMICAL | DOSE | TIME | DISEASE |
|---|---|---|---|
| ACRIFLAVIN | 500MG/LITER | 30 MINUTES | BACTERIAL |
| METHYLENE BLUE | 50MG/LITER | 15 SECONDS | FUNGUS |
| MALACHITE GREEN | 50MG/LITER | 1 MINUTE | FUNGUS |
| FURAN (Furanace) | 1MG/LITER | 10 MINUTES | BACTERIAL |
| GLACIAL ACETIC ACID | 1ML/LITER | 30 SECONDS | PARASITES |
| HYDROGEN PEROXIDE(3%) | 15ML/LITER | 15 MINUTES | PARASITES |
| CHLORAMINE T | 10MG/LITER | 50 MINUTES | BACTERIAL |
| QUININE HCL | 30MG/LITER | 70 MINUTES | PARASITES |
| SODIUM CHLORIDE(SALT) | 0.05% | 1 MONTH | PARASITES |

(Use 4 pounds salt per each 100 gallons of water).

etc., can be applied directly to the wound. By keeping the injured fish in a holding tank, cut off from all light to limit its movements, you can apply the treatment to the wounded site several times a day. This sort of treatment is VERY effective.

This treatment is also suitable after operations.

## Medicated Bath

A very successful method of treating unknown internal parasites and bacterial infections is to put the affected fish into a holding tank which has been medicated. The length of time in which the fish stays in the bath is determined by the primary suggested treatment. The drugs of choice for the 10 minute or shorter bath are formalin, strong salt solution, dyes like methylene blue, acriflavine, gentian violet, malachite green and a strong concentration of water-soluble terramycin. Long-term baths of 2-3 days usually utilize a weak salt solution, potassium permanganate, sulfa drugs, water-soluble antibiotics (which have to be renewed every 24 hours or less) and furan-based drugs.

When fishes are placed into any medicated bath they must be carefully observed so they can be removed if they show urgent stress by jumping, rolling onto their sides, falling to the bottom or thrashing

Fishes without scales like the German carp or doitsu strain of koi are more apt to have parasites and skin conditions than other fishes. Fishes with very white skins sometimes get discolored when bathed in dyes. Photo by Hugh Nicholas.

violently. For this reason prepare a reserve emergency holding tank (the author uses two 55 gallon garbage bags, one inside the other, half filled with aged water).

After the treatment, fishes should be maintained in the holding tank until they appear normal once again.

If repeated medicated baths don't relieve the symptoms, but the fish is still alive and active, then you may have made an incorrect diagnosis, or the fish was permanently damaged internally and cannot be brought back to perfect health. Many cripples live a long life!

There are many other chemicals and drugs recommended in the literature. Some chemicals mentioned in the literature, such as malathion, are too toxic, too expensive or too difficult to find. The suggested treatments are just as good.

**A healthy fish looks like a healthy fish even if you know nothing about them. This is a young red ryukin goldfish. Photo by Fred Rosenzweig.**

### Injections

The diagnosis of a bacterial infection would indicate treatment via injection. The recommended antibiotic or sulfa drug is injected into the fish's abdominal cavity being careful not to hit any vital organs, or into the fish's muscle on the dorsal edge or anterior to the anal pore.

Some specialists are even able to find the large vein in the fish's tail and give it an intravenous injection. Essentially, injections must be given by experts because the dosage must be exact and the drugs must be available. If you are lucky enough to find a veterinarian who specializes in fishes (and you can afford his services), let the vet do it.

An accurate diagnosis is necessary before injection therapy commences.

### Operations

Fishes have been used as laboratory animals for a long time. The author used fishes in his study of melanoma (black skin cancer) and that's how he became interested in fishes. Now surgeons are turning their attention to fishes...mostly as practice before they move on to higher animals...and eventually humans.

Large lumps on the sides of koi usually indicate an ovarian tumor. This is operable. Believe it or not, fish surgeons have successfully removed the diseased eyes from koi and replaced them with glass eyes! Of course only one eye per fish is possible to be replaced or the fish will be blind. The glass eye is merely for aesthetic purposes.

# RECOGNIZING FISH DISEASE HIGHLIGHTS

1. The usual way beginners recognize fish disease is when the fish can barely swim, lies on the bottom or dies. It is essential that you learn to recognize when your fishes' health is compromised.

2. You must learn what a normal fish looks like so you can recognize an abnormal condition such as torn fins, ulcers, tiny white spots or a bulging head or belly.

3. All fish parasites are easily curable, especially the external parasites, providing they are treated early enough. The internal parasites usually require a specialist.

4. The atypical (unusual) social behavior is the first sign of most fish diseases. Koi should school when they swim; if they don't then there is a problem waiting to be solved.

5. You need a holding tank, magnifying glass and flashlight to help recognize external parasites. General cures usually kill all external parasites.

6. If fishes don't breathe normally, stop eating and stop swimming, you have a serious health problem on your hands. Breathing problems almost always are problems with the gills.

7. The five methods of treating fish diseases are oral administration via medicated feed, applying drugs directly at the wound site, medicated baths, injections and operations.

8. There are many drug and chemical choices for medicated baths. You MUST select the correct treatment or the bath is worthless.

9. Because surgeons are now practicing on fish like koi, we can expect many advances in surgical treatment for tumors and the other surgically treated problems.

# The Recognition of Pond Fish Diseases by Their Symptoms

The vast majority of pond fish diseases are recognizable by the educated beginner. (An educated beginner is one who has studied this book!) So, while most fish disease books categorize diseases by the causative agents (like bacteria, viruses, external parasites, etc.), this book will deal with symptoms. Keep in mind that treating symptoms is not treating the disease. So if the disease is stress-caused by a bad environment, you have to clean up the environment or you haven't cured the disease.

Almost all diseases of pond fish are related to water and feed. There is NO substitute for changing the water about 5% per day minimum. In running water like this, it is doubtful you will ever have an acute disease. But you might have long term diseases from bad feed.

Here are the symptoms and their treatments.

## WHITE SPOT DISEASE (ICH)

A few small spots, about the size of a pin prick, usually first noticeable on the fins, is found to spread all over the fish's body. The white spot is the dormant stage of the free-swimming *Ichthyophthirius multifiliis*. This disease is so common it has the popular name *Ich*. Almost every aquarium fish may fall prey to this parasite. In its egg shape it has a length of 0.7mm.

There are many treatments for this disease. The usual method is to place the infected fish in a holding tank. Raise the temperature to about 85°F or even as high as 88°F. Your pet shop will have lots of Ich remedies and they will probably be successful in treating the problem. Under treatment, the white spots disappear within 4-7 days. The reason for raising the temperature is to get the white spots to hatch into free-swimming adults so that the chemicals can be productive.

Most professionals use salt as a cure for Ich. In large tanks or ponds, copper sulfate or methylene blue is used. Salt is the best cure because it is the least toxic. You want non-iodized salt. Add 2 tablespoonfuls to each 5 tablespoonful per 5 gallons. Neither koi nor goldfish should have any problem with this concentration of salt. Keep treating the fish for 48 hours after all the white spots have disappeared. It is not uncommon for the Ich parasites to have dug into the skin under the fish's scales and not be reached by the salt treatment.

Ich only attacks fish under stress. In a tropical aquarium, when Ich strikes, it usually strikes all the fish of one species, not touching the other species. This is because certain species of fishes have a lower level of resistance to stress.

This firemouth cichlid, *Cichlasoma meeki*, is peppered with white spot disease caused by the parasite *Ichthyopthirius multifiliis*. Photo by Dieter Untergasser.

gallons of water EVERY DAY. Change 25% of the water every other day, that is 48 hours after you have started the salt bath. If the fish show signs of discomfort immediately place them into water without salt and cut the salt concentration to one

Not all fishes get Ich. Because some fishes seem to be immune to Ich, scientists have developed a vaccine against Ich. This vaccine has yet to be approved by the FDA because its intended use is to treat catfish being raised for food. Catfish are especially

White spot disease, ich, is characterized by white spots over the fins and body of the infected fish. Drawn by John Quinn.

susceptible to Ich damage because they have no protective scales.

### RAISED SCALES

This symptom is very important because it is so easily recognized by beginners. In Japan the koi farmers refer to *raised scale disease* as *pine cone disease* because the fish appear as a pine cone with their scales standing perpendicular to the body instead of lying flat.

Nobody knows the cause of pine cone disease; there are many reasons for the disease occurring and all of them have different origins. Essentially when the pockets in which the scales are anchored fill with a liquid, the scales begin to rise. This always happens in a small area at first, and then spreads. When this happens the fish is said to have *dropsy*.

Another symptom of dropsy is the swelling of the abdomen. The causes of the abdominal swelling may be a tumor, bleeding viscera or the reaction of a wound and thus it will either disappear in a few weeks or the fish will perish.

Since 1974 there has been an annual outbreak of dropsy in the huge breeding areas in Japan where koi farms are the main source of income in the area. It only occurs in the early summer when the rains are heavy. Usually the 3 month old fish start to turn white and the rear half of their body swells, causing the scales to rise. In 1974 it caused the death of 45% of the fish yearlings in some areas. Each year fewer and fewer yearlings died, indicating that the survivors were becoming immune to whatever caused the dropsy.

The farmers with whom I have spoken said that they only have the problems when their pond water turns muddy brown. Many Japanese scientists have studied the problem and have found no specific cause.

In 63% of the cases studied, fishes with dropsy there had infections of virus, bacteria and/or such parasites as *Hexamita*. The internal organs bleed and may fill the abdomen with a bloody discharge which increases the activities of infectious organisms already within the viscera of the host fish.

Abdominal dropsy is easily recognized once you are familiar with the protruding scales. The bulging eyes are also symptomatic of dropsy. The Japanese call this *pine cone disease* because the fish has the appearance of a pine cone. Photo by Dieter Untergasser,

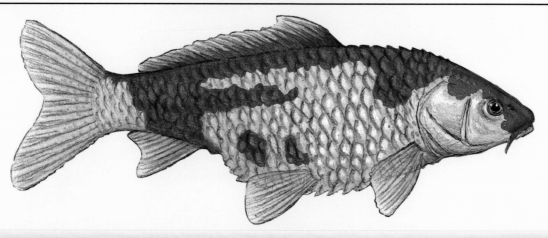

**A koi with dropsy showing protruding scales. Drawn by John Quinn.**

**This goldfish has dropsy. It is often confused by the beginner with pearl scale development, especially in rounded goldfish. Photo by Fred Mertlich.**

The answer is simple: NO ONE KNOWS FOR SURE WHAT CAUSES DROPSY IN FISH. Everyone who studies this problem agrees that there are several causes. Most people who work with the fish are convinced a typical salt treatment seems to help.

Where bacterial invaders may be the cause, an antibiotic bath may work at times. When the *Herpes* virus attacks the fish and the scales

rise, the fish seldom dies but cures itself since we have no cures for viral infections in fishes at the moment.

So isolate the dropsical fish in a quarantine tank, treat it with salt and antibiotic and hope for the best. It is not known whether dropsy is contagious because no one is sure of what causes it. To be safe, isolate all infected fish. It is unheard of that ALL the fishes in a given pond develop dropsy.

**A goldfish with dropsy.**

Sometimes local infections cause a localized swelling which may result in localized scale protrusions. This is not dropsy and the scales will return to normal when the infection has been cured.

## EXTENDED GILL COVERS

This disease is sometimes referred to in Japan as *swollen cheek disease*. It is a disease of young fish, about one month old, but it also affects older fish. The gills of the infected fish are open as wide as the fish can get them. This discloses very red gills. Gills, like the fish's skin, are subject to infection by many diseases because they are always in contact with pond water.

Gills perform several major functions. The fish's gills excrete nitrogenous waste material. They give off carbon dioxide (from the blood) and take in oxygen. Each gill arch is constructed of what are called *primary lamellae*. If you look at one of these lamellae under a microscope (at about 25X natural size) you will see rows of secondary lamellae. All of these should have a healthy intense reddish color; light-color gills are a sure sign of disease or anemia (which is also a disease). When we talk about gill color we mean the color when the fish is alive. When a fish dies its gills pale because the blood flows out of them. The most common

A pom-pon goldfish with the genetic defect of extended gill cover, often called *swollen cheek* disease. Photo by Fred Rosenzweig.

water is hard or soft. Instructions usually come with the chemical. As an example at pH6.0, in soft water, you use 2.5mg/liter. The same water pH but hard water, and you need 7.0mg/liter. At a pH of 8.0 you need 20.0mg/liter in soft water and the same in hard water.

The treatment with chloramine-T should be repeated every 4 hours (using new water for each bath) over a 16 hour period (four baths). This is a very effective treatment.

According to the Japanese koi farmers, they use koi that are 2 years old and have been grown outdoors in their large ponds. These fish are sacrificed and ground up alive. The meat is fed to the koi in the pond, every day for a week. This, they say, immunizes the yearlings against swollen cheek disease.

problems observed when gills are closely examined are *swollen gills*, medically called *hypertrophy* and *hyperplasia*. The hypertrophic gill shows enlargement of the lamellae themselves, while the hyperplastic gill shows enlargement of the cells in the gill but the cells are otherwise normal.

Hyperplasia and hypertrophy are the symptoms of attacks of protozoans, especially *Chilodonella* and *Trichodina*. Ich only causes hyperplasia around the site of their attachment.

Infestation by the parasitic protozoan *Amblyoodinium ocellatum* is also well known in aquacultural circles.

The best overall treatment is the use of chloramine-T (N-Chloro-4-Methylbenzenesulfonamide Sodium). The amount of drug to use is dependent on the quantity of water and the pH of that water and whether the

Extended gill covers, or *swollen cheek disease*, is a symptom of several diseases. The gills must be examined for parasites; best treatment for all of the diseases which cause extended gill covers is chloramine-T.

**Body fungus, probably caused by *Saprolegnia*, always follows a stressful situation in which the fish's immune system fails.**

**Goldfish showing fungus infections. Fungus infections are almost always secondary infections since the fungus live on dead tissue.**

**Body fungus resulting from torn fins during a stressful netting of the fish.**

Fungus is a cotton-like growth which the Japanese also call *water mold* and *cotton cover*. Fungus growths are symptoms of several basic infections. Fungi on fishes usually belong to the genera *Saprolegnia*, *Leptomitus*, and *Pythium*. It doesn't matter at all to which genus the fungus (mold) belongs, as they are treated identically.

Certain parasitic infections, especially *Flavobacterium* and *Epistylis*, look like typical *Saprolegnia* infections, but they aren't. Again it doesn't matter, for the treatment of all fungus-like infections is the same.

*Saprolegnia* is the common scientific name applied to all fungus infections on fishes *whether or not the identification has actually been ascertained.*

In actual fact there are many water molds in the class Oomycetes which look macroscopically like *Saprolegnia*. Many attack fishes. Water molds are different from non-water molds because the water molds need water to transmit their spores. Land molds produce aerial spores. The spores travel around in cysts (like little eggs) hoping to find a suitable site upon which the spores can germinate (hatch) and root. The spores of the water molds can only germinate on DEAD tissue (that's what the *sapro* part of the name means...*dead*) and they are called *saprophytes*. What all this means to the pond fish keeper is that their fish has to have dead tissue open to infection or there will be no fungus infection. Healthy fish which are not wounded

**A champion red cap goldfish which has, unfortunately, been attacked by an infection in the cap. The infection is being complicated with fungus. Photo by Fred Rosenzweig.**

gets a foothold through the skin of the fish, it quickly spreads across the skin. Typically, though, if a fin is wounded, the fungus is more limited to the initial site of infection because of the lack of musculature in the fin itself.

The mycelia are the cottony threads by which we recognize the fungus infection. Initially, in clean, clear water, these mycelia are white. Due to chemicals, algae and debris in the water, the fine mycelia often change color to represent that they have trapped these elements. It takes time for the mycelia to do this, thus a fine white fungus growth means a fresh attack; if the color has changed, the attack took place days earlier. This is important because it is best to catch the fungus growth at the initial site of infection where it can be swabbed with malachite green or a supersaturated salt (sodium chloride, non-iodized) solution.

Treatments are simple. Both non-iodized table salt and malachite green work wonderfully well if the site of infection is small. The larger the affected area, the smaller the chance for the fish's survival.

Many people eat koi because they are, after all, just fancy colored carp and carp have been cultured and eaten for many centuries. If you intend to eat your koi, don't use malachite green to treat them.

The next best treatment is an extended bath in a low salt solution. Using a holding tank with a heater (set for 80°F) and a sponge filter for

cannot get a fungus infection. Fish allowed to remain in the water after they have died will be completely covered with fungus in a few days.

Fungus can also grow on things in the water besides fish. Overfeeding can result in the fungus growing on the uneaten food. Fungus are associated with dirty water conditions. The dirty water causes a breakdown in the fish's normal immunosuppressive system. This allows external parasites, bacterial and viral infections to attack the skin of the fish. The site of the attack produces dead tissue and this dead tissue is a perfect

hatchery for the water mold spores. Wounds, even on perfectly healthy fishes in a perfectly healthy environment, can also be attacked by water mold. However in clean, running water fishes with fungus (water mold) infections are very rare. In dirty water they are very common.

The most common immunosuppressive factor with pond fishes is a sudden large temperature drop in their pond or aquarium water. Since water molds do better in lower water temperatures (below 50°F) than they do at the higher more normal pond temperatures, the combination often proves fatal to fishes. Once the fungus

aeration, add 2-3 pounds of salt per 100 gallons. One hundred gallons is the recommended size for a holding (quarantine) tank. Use the dosage of two pounds of salt for a fast treatment. If the fungus infection is not a fungus but *Epistylis* or *Flavobacterium*, it will cure within a week. Other infections may take longer, so

by fungus. The fungus spreads, opening up more sites for bacterial infection, etc. That's why you might add an antibiotic to the holding tank. Try 250mg of water soluble tetracycline or terramycin for each 5 gallons of water EVERY DAY.

Malachite green is a dye. It is the best treatment for fungus infections on fishes

Swab the infected area using a strong solution of 100 mg per liter. Malachite green is such a strong dye that it colors most things with which it is in contact, even plastics.

To summarize: Fungus molds are ever present. They cannot be eliminated from the water environment. They are saprophytes which means

Fungus appearing on the body of a koi is usually caused by injuries which have become infected. The infection, by bacteria, produces dead tissue upon which the fungus grow. Drawn by John Quinn.

add the additional pound of salt over a few days. If you change 5% of the water in the holding tank daily (a 25% daily water change is even better), be sure to add enough salt to maintain the specific gravity of the solution. If you have a hydrometer (pet shops use them for testing the salinity of their marine fish tanks), you are shooting for a 1.030 reading (= a 0.03% saline solution).

There is a horrible bacteria-fungus-bacteria cycle. The bacteria infect a wound site. The infection kills some tissue which is immediately infected

or on fish eggs. Methylene blue may also be used, but malachite green is better. BE WARNED: Malachite green is poisonous if you breathe in the powder. It may cause cancer (in humans), and its effect may be cumulative (in your skin as well as the fish's). Use rubber gloves and a face mask when handling malachite green. You are advised to use salt, but malachite green is more efficacious. As a bath for an extended period of time, use 0.10 mg of malachite green per liter of water. Change the solution every 8 hours.

they can only reproduce on dead organic matter. They cannot attack an unwounded healthy fish. They can attack a fish whose immunosuppressive system has failed because of temperature stress (sudden large drop in water temperature) or filthy water environment. The faster you see and treat the fungus infection, the better are the fish's chances of survival. Malachite green is the best treatment for the fish but is dangerous (to you); salt is safer (for you), thus it is the recommended treatment.

ULCER DISEASE, FINROT, TAILROT, GILLROT, MOUTHROT, COLUMNARIS DISEASE, COTTON WOOL DISEASE, MYXOBACTERIAL DISEASE.

This family of diseases almost looks like a fungus infection except the mycelia are missing and it is a flat, gray mass.

This is a bacterial infection caused by stress due to bad water where the immunosuppressive system has been compromised. The slightest injury to the weakened fish establishes a site for the infection by *columnaris*.

Scientifically, *columnaris* had been placed in many genera until it was finally located in the genus *Flexibacter* as *Flexibacter columnaris*.

The formation of shallow ulcers gets progressively worse as it reddens, expands and kills the skin tissue, often inviting a true water mold invasion. The skin and gills often exude a thick yellow slime, which, when on the gills, is called *gill rot.*

This infection is incorrectly called a myxobacterial infection and usually only attacks freshwater fishes in ponds at higher than 55 °F water temperature. It is highly infectious and usually attacks the external surfaces of the fish (skin, fins) as well as the gills. The lesions form easily when fish are under stress, and the lesions quickly develop ulcers which have peripheries of yellowish orange. The ulceration deepens and the fish has its blood infected with *columnaris*. Deep ulcers are rarely treatable.

In gill rot, the *columnaris* attacks the ends of the lamellae causing their destruction. They keep attacking the gill lamellae

1. The disease from Mag Noy in Israel, which has been brought under control, manifested itself with fin rot (dorsal fin) and an ulcer at the base of the ventral fins. Photos by Dr. Herbert R. Axelrod.
2. Another ulcer diseased goldfish from Mag Noy.
3. Many fish heal themselves from ulcer disease. You can easily see where the ulceration healed over.
4. Lymphocystis disease is impossible for the beginner to properly diagnose, but it is often confused with ulcer disease. It is commonly called *cotton wool disease*. Drawn by John Quinn.

**4**

until there are no gill lamellae left.

This disease attacked goldfish from Israel in 1994. They developed the so-called *Ulcer Disease* and every goldfish shipped from Mag Noy Goldfish Farm (the largest in Israel) developed an ulcer. The successful treatment recognized that the goldfish became ill only after they were subjected to water above 55°F. Once the fish were bathed in potassium permanganate for a week before they were shipped, the disease disappeared.

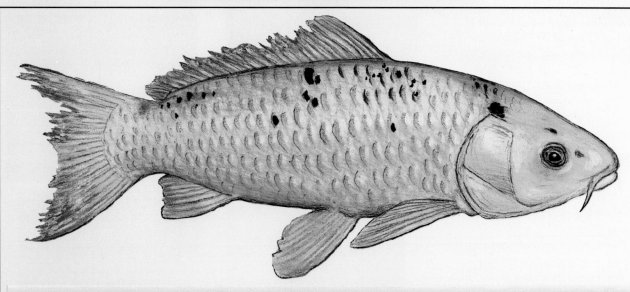

Fin rot is the gradual degradation of the fins from disease, injury and/or malnutrition. It is easily treated but the cure requires the cause to be corrected. Drawn by John Quinn.

This koi jumped out of the pond onto a concrete surface where it flapped around for a few minutes before it was thrown back into the pond. The slime coating and scales were injured and the fish suffered this cotton wool fungus. Photo by K. Murakami.

Treatments with antibiotic feeds (containing tetracycline especially) are very successful if the fish are eating. Very often they stop eating (anorexia) and oral medications cannot be administered. In this case they should be bathed in potassium permanganate or copper sulfate. Experimental treatments with oxytetracycline have been successful, but potassium permanganate is the best

Mouth fungus usually follows an injury and subsequent bacterial infection of the lips. The inset shows a live fish with a bacterial mouth infection. Drawn by John Quinn. Photo by MP&C Piednoir Aqua Press.

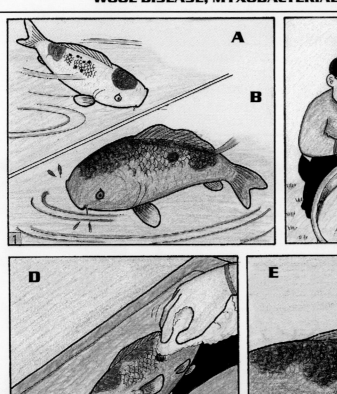

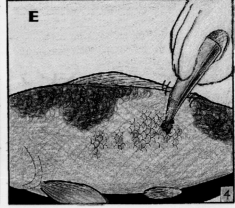

(A) In cases of ulcer disease, you must recognize the problem as quickly as possible. (B) If the ulcer is large, the problem is more difficult. (C) Put the fish to sleep with any fish anaesthesia. (D) Lay the fish on an absorbent towel and dry the side of the fish which has to be treated. (E) Using tweezers and a sharp knife remove the fungused area and scrape away surrounding tissue and scales even if they look healthy. Sterilize the instruments in between uses. (F) Apply antibiotic, mercurochrome, iodine, or any other remedy which your local pet shop might recommend. Repeat this treatment at least twice a day for a week. (G) Place the fish into an antibiotic bath for a week or so. It should heal. Drawings courtesy of RINKO magazine.

because its use has been so refined.

A fast dip for 30 seconds in a bath containing 1 gram of potassium permanganate per liter of water is recommended for starters when only a few individual fish are involved. For a bath of one hour use a concentration of 5 mg per liter of water. Use fresh, but aged, aquarium water.

Where a whole pond is infected, start with adding one gram per 100 gallons. This should turn the water slightly pink. If, within 30 minutes, the pink coloration disappears, add 10% more of the initial dosage, wait another 30 minutes, and see if the pink color stabilizes. Keep adding potassium permanganate until the pink color is stable after 30 minutes. By the time the color fades, the fishes should either be cured or dead.

It is absolutely necessary for treating this disease, and just about every other disease, to practice sound pond water sanitation. After a day or two of treatment with potassium permanganate, start to change all of the pond water at the rate of 25% per day. Be sure the tank or pond is clean and kept that way. Most harmful diseases are aided by poor aquatic environment when a fish's immunosuppressive system is compromised

**A goldfish starting an ulcer disease.**

**This koi died of wasting disease. Its dorsal fin was completely eaten away by bacteria. Antibiotic bath would have solved the problem quickly. Photo by MP&C Piednoir Aqua Press.**

(A) Capture the fish to be treated in the potassium permanganate bath (or any chemical bath for that matter) and hold them in a plastic bag until you are ready to treat them. (B) Using gloves to protect yourself, dissolve the potassium permanganate in boiling water. (C) Add the super-saturated solution of potassium permanganate to the holding tank (=quarantine tank or hospital tank). (D) Stir it vigorously to be sure the chemical is diluted and evenly spread. It should be light purple. (E) Take the bag with the koi and add them (and the waterin which they came) to the holding tank after you are sure the water is about the same temperature. (F)Use an aerator during the treatment regardless of the total time necessary for the bath. Drawings courtesy of RINKO magazine.

The little animals they call copepods are very plentiful. There are at least 9,750 different species in many different families. These animals are easy to culture so they are favorites of university students working in the field. Every student seems to find a few new species to reward his efforts. Of the 9,750 species more than 1,500 are parasitic. Of these 1,500 parasitic copepods, about 1,250 only affect marine fishes while the balance of about 250 species attacks freshwater fishes. To properly identify the copepod attacking your fish requires an experienced parasitologist who works in the field of parasitic copepods. Since the treatment for all of these parasitic copepods is the same, the identification doesn't really matter. In the aquarium trade, the anchor worms are usually assigned to *Lernaea cyprinacea*, but there are many other possibilities. The copepods are about 10 mm long (there are 25.4 mm to an inch), so they are easily seen in the proper light. If there are only a few, they can be removed with tweezers, with the wound swabbed with iodine. If there are more than a few or you don't want to swab, then bathe the fish in a 0.03% solution of non-iodized salt mixed with aged but fresh water. The fish can soak in

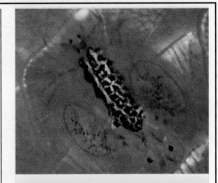

**A fish louse. There are many kinds of fish lice, but they can all be treated the same way with removal with tweezers and a salt bath.**

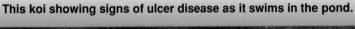

**This koi showing signs of ulcer disease as it swims in the pond.**

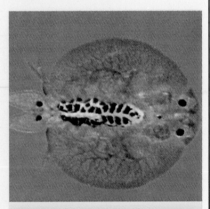

*Argulus*, **the fish louse. Photo by Dr. E. Elkan.**

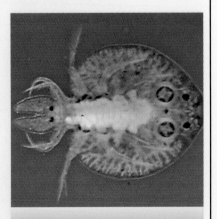

**A fish louse.**

this bath for a week or until they show signs of discomfort. Use a hydrometer to be sure the specific gravity is 1.030. The treatment should be accomplished in a holding tank where there is aeration, filtration and a heater (set for 70°F).

Sometimes the copepods attach to the gill arches, the inside of the mouth or the skin where they may raise welts which are red and dangerous looking. Properly treated anchor worms are not life threatening. But if they grow extensively on a fish or if the fish is small, the debilitation could result in the fish's death.

A newer treatment for anchor worm is organophosphates. A long term bath of 1 mg/gallon of trichlorfon (organophosphate). Keep temperature below 75°F. Repeat the treatment every week for four weeks.

Some writers warn against using organophosphates to treat European pond fishes like rudd and orfe. The present author has no personal experience with this fatal encounter.

**WARNING** A judge in London, England, ruled that a farm worker had been damaged by organophosphate poisoning. Organophosphates were originally developed as nerve gas agents, but they are used by farmers throughout the world as insecticides and pesticides. They are very effective and are often found in household products. **YOU HAVE BEEN WARNED!**

*Lernaea cyprinacea*, the anchor worm, on the skin of goldfish. Photo by Frickhinger.

### FISH LICE, *ARGULUS*, BRANCHIURAN INFECTION

This is a disease of all pond fish. They don't have to be suffering from any other disease or weakened by infections. Perfectly healthy fish can be parasitized by fish lice in the genus *Argulus*. This parasite seems to be specific for goldfish and koi as they are almost the only fish infected. These nasty little branchiurans attack a fish and immediately attach themselves via two sucking devices. Then they lance the fish with their stinger. Under the microscope (low power about 20X) the mouth can be seen to be the stinger itself. It acts like a mosquito, squirting in a digestive enzyme which makes the blood or other body fluid liquid enough to be sucked up by the stinger. After an hour or so of sucking the area dry, it moves a little

Anchor worm, *Lernaea*, attached to a koi. Note the swelling at the point of attachment.

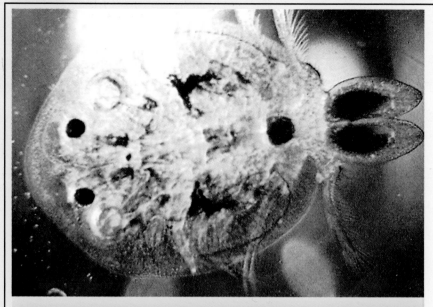

This is the *Argulus* fish parasite which, when fully mature, is easily seen with the naked eye. Its large size makes it easily removable with a tweezers. Photo by W. Tomey.

ABOVE: A goldfish showing symptoms of an anchor worm infection. Photo by Erik L. Johnson, DVM.

BELOW: This goldfish recovered from wounds inflicted by fish lice.

The legs of the parasite are also equipped with holdfasts, like a fly, to insure their security as the *Argulus* feeds.

*Argulus*, like mosquitoes, can carry diseases. Their sites of penetration often become infected with bacteria and eventually water mold (fungus) as a secondary invader. Treatment of the *Argulus* must be fast and decisive. If bacterial infections have already set in as indicated by red circular ulcers, the fish must also be treated for these problems.

Ordinarily a few *Argulus* on a large koi or goldfish are not a problem, but the *Argulus* are champion breeders. One parasite can have 500 offspring in a month!

The treatment is simple. Remove as many parasites as you can find with tweezers. Swab each site with iodine. Then treat the fish to an organophosphate bath using 0.25 mg of trichlorfon per liter, or use 0.50 mg per liter if the temperature is over 75°F. Use this treatment every week for four weeks. A 0.03% salt solution is also effective in many cases. In all cases isolate the fish into a holding tank with aeration and heat.

Some authorities warn that salt treatments, like organophosphate treatments, may be fatal to rudd, orfe and other European pond fishes. That has not been my experience.

As with all diseases, the sooner the problem is discovered, the easier it is to cure. You can only discover fish problems if the fish are visible and you are looking at them! That's one of the advantages of having the pond fish eat out of your hand.

and jabs the fish again. The toxic enzymes injected into the fish cause an itching which becomes evident as the fish rubs against rocks, walls, the pond or aquarium bottom.

The white spots on the cheeks of this goldfish merely show that the fish is a male in breeding dress! It is NOT a symptom of disease.
INSET: Pulling out anchor worms with tweezers. It is best to anesthetize the fish before doing this. Photo courtesy of RINKO magazine.

The breeder of this fish, Megumi Yoshida, raised koi together with the author on a farm in Florida in 1965. Mr. Yoshida still has a koi farm in Japan. His address is NISHIKIGOI YOSHIDA CO., 646 TENJINSHITA-YAHO,KUNITACHI, TOKYO, JAPAN (phone 0425-73-4158. The fish is a gin-rin prize winner at the 26th Tokyo Koi Show. It is now owned by Shigekatsu Takahashi.

A koi or goldfish which struggles to the surface of the water only to slowly sink down again, where it may even land upside down, is said to have swim bladder disease. Japanese and older English books on fish diseases list the cause as indigestion. The indigestion causes the intestines to swell. The swollen intestines press against the swim bladder and, if the swim bladder has a fatty degeneration problem and has no room to swell, the bladder might rupture. Once the bladder ruptures there is no cure, of course.

The same phenomenon occurs with roundworm infection of the swim bladder by the nematode *Anguillicola*.

The treatment of swim bladder disease caused by roundworms (nematodes) requires the use of antihelminthics such as piperazine, fenbendazole and levamisole. These are effective against the adult forms. The eggs (cysts) cannot be treated. The infected fish must be fed 5 mg of piperazine sulfate for each pound of body weight each day for 3 days. Treatment should be in a holding tank. If the fish doesn't eat try the intubation of fenbendazole, 25 mg per pound of fish body weight. Of course you can always inject the fish with 3.6 mg of levamisole hydrochloride intracardiac. Don't try this if you're not expert at fish injections!

## SWOLLEN BELLY, TUMORS OF THE REPRODUCTIVE ORGANS

Fat koi with bulging bellies are a problem because there are at least a dozen conditions which can make a koi's belly

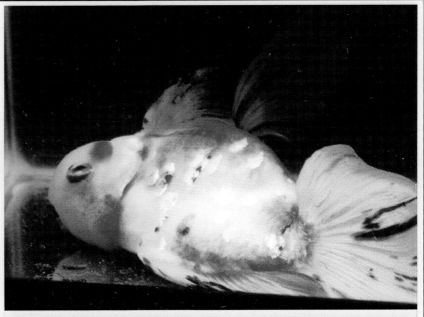

Oranda goldfish suffering from bloat, ends up on the bottom of the tank unable to swim. Photo by Erik L. Johnson, DVM.

Bubble-eyed goldfish always suffer some injuries to their bubbles as you can see from the wound marks on the bubble (right side).

bulge. We have already discussed the fatty degeneration of the liver syndrome which causes the whole abdomen to fill with fat. This is caused by poor food. But there are many organic disorders which cause a koi's belly to distend. In these problems the scales do not stick out like a pine cone.

A common cause of swollen belly is a tumor of the ovaries in the female or a tumor of any other visceral organ. Oftentimes the belly fills with pus, or, when the kidneys fail, the belly fills with liquid. You can only be sure of what's going on by surgical observation. Just cut the koi's belly open and look.

The cost of doing this and the possibility of the fish surviving the surgery and the treatment are arguments against doing anything. Change the fish's diet and hope that its fatty liver will go away with proper diet. You can treat for abscesses with antibiotics but you are really shooting in the dark.

DON'T CONFUSE A FEMALE HEAVY WITH EGGS WITH A DISEASED FISH!!

**A nice koi in trouble from abdominal distension which may have been caused by fatty liver degeneration, tumor of the ovaries or some visceral infection. The scales are not distended. The disease is usually fatal.**

When a female is bulging with eggs, usually in the spring, the eggs can be gently squeezed out of her by someone experienced in doing this (most koi are bred this way). Or else leave the fish alone. If it doesn't cure itself by proper diet, you'll find out what it died from upon autopsy.

## GAS BUBBLE DISEASE

Gas supersaturation is known as gas bubble disease in the pond fish trade. It can occur under many circumstances that are all mechanical. Essentially it makes too much dissolved air in the pond water available to the fishes. The fishes trap the air in bubbles throughout their bodies, including but not limited to the blood system, the skin, the eyes, the gills, every internal organ. The treatment is simply to remove the source of the excess air. This may be a Venturi effect on a water outlet emptying into your pond, too much turbulence from an air stone or air releaser, a water fountain that is too active and, most importantly, a dramatic increase in water temperature. The increased temperature forces the water to give up the air it contains. This air may settle on the fishes. The usual source of this warm water is from a home's water supply where the hose was hooked up to the hot water instead of the cold water, or, where the mix was made incorrectly and the water gets hotter and hotter.

For the warm water problem simply add cooler water or ice to the pond as quickly as possible.

There are mechanical devices to protect against gas bubble disease. The best of them are called *packed column degassers*. They are usually not available from pet shops. They are made by Aquatic Ecosystems, Inc., 2056 Apopka Boulevard, Apopka, Florida 32703. Contact them for further information about cost, function and availability

**Koi people often call the distended belly, the *bloat*. Unquestionably this fish is bloated. Drawn by John Quinn.**

For some unknown reason, as koi become emaciated, they lose the musculature along their back. This bilateral dystrophy (shrinking both sides of the dorsal edge uniformly) progresses until the fish doesn't have enough muscle to enable it to swim. The fish looks and acts pathetically.

Amazingly, they are very active. They swim with the school of other koi until they cannot swim any longer. They eat sparingly. There is no known cure and no known cause. The Japanese literature is very vague reporting a loss of body fat, a similarity to men's sugar diabetes and lack of real success with Vitamin E treatment.

This doesn't seem to be a nutritional problem since it is usually unique among the inhabitants of a water garden. The few cases investigated by the author indicated the fish were raised in dirt bottom ponds or pools in an unsanitary condition. But since more than 93% of the koi are pond raised, this is not a conclusive observation.

### HOLE-IN-THE-HEAD DISEASE

A special disease occurs in larger koi which has been described as hole-in-the-head disease. Small pits occur, usually on the head, but also along the lateral line. It affects koi, most large cichlids (especially *Symphysodon*, the discus fish), and marine tangs and marine angelfish. As time goes on, the hole gets larger and larger and usually becomes infected with *Aeromonas* and *Epistylis*. *Aeromonas* is a typical bacterial infection which,

when untreated, results in the death of the untreated fish. *Epistylis* is a protozoan parasite that is associated with *Aeromonas* because it eats it! *Epistylis* is a feeder on bacteria and is found where there is high bacterial activity be it on the body of a fish or in the water. Its appearance on fishes seems to be merely a convenient holdfast or anchoring site.

Treatment of hole-in-the-head disease varies from surgical cleansing of the sites

This koi is affected by sekoke disease, the name by which the Japanese refer to wasting disease or razor back. Photo courtesy of RINKO magazine.

to treatment with Calcipot (calcium plus phosphorus and vitamins D and E; made by Hoechst) and Osspulvit (a multivitamin and trace

element combination; made by Hoechst). The most encouraging reports on hole-in-the-head disease comes from Dieter Untergasser in his exceptional book *HANDBOOK OF FISH DISEASES* (TS-123 published by T.F.H.).

Treatment for the bacterial and protozoan infection helps the general health of the fish, as does the usual 0.03% salt bath routine. The Japanese report that kanamycin injections are remarkably effective.

### FLUKES, MONOGENEANS

There is a large group of microscopic worms which are gathered together under the common names of Eye Flukes, Gill Flukes, Skin Flukes, and under such scientific names as *Gyrodactylus* and *Dactylogyrus*. These names are famous, as are *Costia*, *Pseudomonas*, *Chilodonella* and *Trichodina*. They all mean trouble for koi and goldfish. They all require microscopes and an education in parasite identification to recognize them and to differentiate one from the other. Once you know how, it is easy, but outside of government-sponsored fish laboratories, it's difficult for a fish pathologist to make a living! Unfortunately it is more cost effective to dispose of sick fish than to cure them except on a fish farming economy. But, if you have a scientific inclination, buy an inexpensive microscope (one that will minimally magnify up to 100X and have a built in or accessory light source), some dyes, slides, etc. (all available from biological supply houses, school

The two holes in the head of this koi indicate it has hole-in-the-head disease. Treatment usually requires surgery to remove the infected tissue, then various baths and antibiotics to control infections resulting from the surgery. Photo by Burkhard Kahl.

suppliers, etc.) Ask your local biology teacher for help! Oftentimes the study of fish diseases is as interesting as the keeping of koi! (It was for me.)

Fortunately for koi and goldfish keepers, there are a host of treatments for flukes and their likes, and all of them are efficacious.

Effective remedies in the literature include baths with benzocaine, toltrazuril, chloramine-T, mebendazole, praziquantel, common table salt (non-iodized), copper sulfate, potassium permanganate, acetic acid, organophosphates, formalin and a special fluke medication sold in pet shops under the name *Fluke Tabs*.

Most of the flukes have hooks, suction disks, anchors, claws and spikes. They eat the mucus (slime) covering the fish's body, suck its blood and vital juices and infect the gills. In later stages they penetrate the fish's external body defenses and the fish ultimately dies from secondary infections.

Fishes constantly rubbing their bodies against solid protuberances in the pond or aquarium, or a thickening of the slime coating, are two sure signs of an infection with monogenean worms. Time is of the essence as most monogeneans are prolific breeders. Most lay eggs, but some are livebearers.

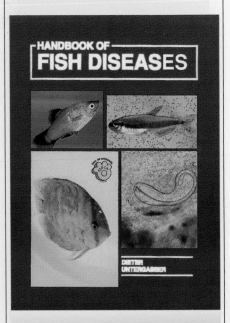

**TS-123**
**Handbook of Fish Diseases**

Treating fish in a small pond or aquarium is best done with Fluke Tabs available from your local pet shop. Use one tablet for each ten gallons of water to be treated. Repeat the treatment 4 days later but change at least 50% of the water before the second treatment.

Potassium permanganate at a dosage of 2 parts per million (=1 gram per 100 gallons) as a 24 hour bath in a holding tank for individual fishes can be used, but the pond or aquarium must be sterilized, too. You can treat the pond with formalin, using 1 cc for each 10 gallons of water. To do this correctly, remove as much water from the pond as easily possible, leaving enough water and aeration to keep the inhabitants alive. Then dose this small amount of water with 1 cc of formalin for each remaining gallon of water. After 2-3 hours (unless the fishes show discomfort), add an equal amount of water to that which was still in the pond. Do this again and again until the pond is full. Then

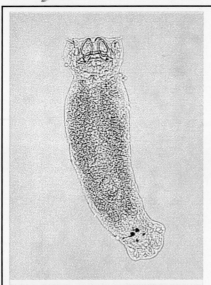

**A gill worm of the Dactylogyridae family is often responsible for gill infections. Photo by Dieter Untergasser.**

start again with the same procedure. Doing this twice should cleanse the pond and the fishes of most flukes.

Keep in mind that formalin is a heavy liquid and very dangerous to your eyes, nose and mouth. Use rubber (or plastic) gloves and a face mask...and be careful. Only apply formalin to water being agitated so that the formalin mixes with the water and dilutes quickly.

If this treatment doesn't work, you might have a different problem. If the salt, Fluke Tabs (which are organophosphates) and formalin treatments fail, you might visit your local veterinarian and get some praziquantel (which is used for small animals under the trade name *Droncit)*. This works very well for treating the fishes in the holding tank. Use 3 mg per liter, three treatments. The first two 48 hours apart, the third one month later. This drug is much too expensive for treating the pond.

## IN CONCLUSION

*If you have read this book through, you have a fair idea of how to recognize and treat the COMMON diseases of koi and goldfish. There are many other diseases and infirmities which affect pond fishes, but they are so rare and so difficult to treat or diagnose as to be unworthy of mention in a book of this sort.*

If you learned anything from this book it should have been: AN OUNCE OF PREVENTION IS WORTH A POUND OF CURE. It is MUCH easier to keep your pond water clean and to feed non-cereal based foods than it is to cure the problems that are caused by bad food and dirty water.

A water garden is like a vegetable garden. It needs attention. The fish keep growing and their needs keep changing as the sunlight becomes weaker or stronger, the fish get larger and baby fish appear mysteriously in the early summer from a spawning which you never knew took place.

Hopefully this is NOT the first book you read about goldfish and koi. The more you know about these colorful and interesting pets, the more you'll want to know. Get involved and join a fish club.

To become more familiar with the subject of fish diseases, get a copy of Dieter Untergasser's *HANDBOOK OF FISH DISEASES*. It is, by far, the best book for aquarists and pond keepers. It is very easy to use and has stood the test of time having been originally published in 1989.

(ISBN 0-86622-703-2; TFH style number TS-123).

## DEDICATION

We all loved our favorite teacher. My fish disease teacher was Dr. Stanislas Snieszko. We studied together and wrote books together. He held nothing back from me or any of his other students or colleagues. He was universally loved and respected. I never heard anyone assail or criticize him. I wish he was still around to read this book before it was published and gently *suggest* that perhaps *this could be written in a better way.* But Stan is gone and this book and every fish disease curative effort may have suffered from his loss.

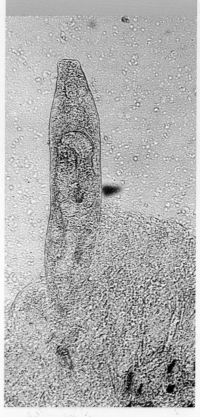

**A gill worm, *Gyrodactylus*, clearing showing it bearing an unborm embryo. Photo by Dieter Untergasser**

# Index